Put God's
Word on Your
WEIGHT

Toni, Put God's word on your weight (All of them) He will move them.

8/11/18

"REAL TALK, STRATEGIC TACTICS WITH DECLARATIONS AND PRAYERS FOR REAL WEIGHT LOSS"

SHARON A. CAREY

All rights reserved sole by the author. The author guarantees all contents are original and do not infringe upon the legal rights of any other person or work. No part of this book may be reproduced, stored in a retrieval system, or transmitted in any form or by any means without expressed written permission of the author.

All quotes, unless otherwise noted, are from the New King James Version. Copyright 1979, 1980, 1982 by Thomas Nelson, Inc. Used by permission. All rights reserved. Scriptures marked KJV are taken from The Holy Bible, King James Version. Public Domain. *Holy Bible,* New Living Translation, copyright © 1996, 2004, 2015 by Tyndale House Foundation. Used by permission of Tyndale House Publishers Inc., Carol Stream, Illinois 60188. All rights reserved. Holy Bible, New International Version®, NIV® Copyright ©1973, 1978, 1984, 2011 by Biblica, Inc.® Used by permission. All rights reserved worldwide.

PUT GOD'S WORD ON YOUR WEIGHT
Real Talk, Strategic Tactics with
Declarations and Prayers for Real Weight Loss

Printed in the USA

To inquiry about inviting Sharon to speak at your church, women's event or conference, please visit Sharon's website or send an email:

Sharon A. Carey
www.sharonacarey.com
Email: info@sharonacarey.com

Copyright ©2018
ISBN 978-1-943343-10-2

DEDICATION

Here's to You!

Put God's Word on Your Weight is dedicated to you! If you have ever experienced the heartache and emotional pain of being overweight, this book was written for you. I can identify with you. I get the pain! I know it! And I feel you.

Praise God! There is help available for those whose battle is weight loss. God has an ointment ready to apply to your wounded soul. When applied consistently, this medicine will work to bring about the physical and inner healing needed to make you whole and well. That medicine is the Word of God. You've tried everything else; now try the medicine of God's Word.

Dedicate this book to yourself and dedicate yourself to this book. Use the strategies, engage in the declarations and prayers, and experience the freedom from weight that can only be given by God.

Yes, this book is dedicated to you, my beloved sister! It is to the overcomer in you, the one who is more than a conqueror through Christ Jesus. Put God's Word on Your Weight and soar like an eagle high above the weight that has kept you caged. I believe you can fly!

Put God's Word on Your Weight

DEEPEST APPRECIATION

Heavenly Father, before one page was written in this book, you called me an author and helped me to accept what you called me. Thank You, Papa! Great is your faithfulness. You are great and greatly to be praised.

Lord Jesus, thank you for the truth that set the captives free! I have come to a greater understanding of the words that you spoke in Mark 9:23 "…Everything is possible for those who believe." Glory to Your Name!

Holy Spirit, my teacher, my friend, and Divine Personal Trainer, thank you for being my counselor through all of this and for the inspiration to write and finish this book. The power of Your presence has amazed me! You have been here through it all.

Michael, my devoted husband and best friend, you have gently carried me through the years and caught me in the spirit. You haven't dropped me, not even once. Your calm spirit has protected my peace and your daily prayer covering strengthens my soul. I thank God for you, my Boaz.

Nina, my daughter, teacher, cheerleader, prayer partner, and friend! You helped me push through the labor pains of this book and all that it took for me to get here. You were the mirror that caused me to see what I was unable to see in myself. Thank you for encouraging me to become what you helped me to see.

Coach Carol Young-Walker, you are a phenomenal trainer! Thank you so much for stretching me. You brought out the physical and mental strength that God gave me for this journey. May the Lord continually add fire to the passion that you have to challenge people to protect their health and to make their bodies their business.

To all my Prayer Warriors who prayed for me to finish what God called me to do, thank you! I could not have done this without the power of your prayers. Please keep praying!

And finally, to my son, family and friends who kept asking, "When are you going to finish that book?" Thank you for being so pushy…I love that about you! Now, how many copies did you say you were getting?

CONTENTS

Introduction vii

Chapter One
  Really, God? 1

Chapter Two
  God Alone 7

Chapter Three
  Counting Losses 13

Chapter Four
  Trans Formed 22

Chapter Five
  The Coach 27

Chapter Six
  The Altar 36

Chapter Seven
  You Are Not The Enemy 42

Chapter Eight
The White Flag 46

Chapter Nine
Say Sow 50

Chapter Ten
The Weight is Over..55

Chapter Eleven
I Believe; Therefore I Speak..59

Put God's Word on Your Weight
Declarations & Prayers for Weight Loss 63

End Notes 80

Introduction

This book may have gotten your attention because you have tried everything in your power to lose weight, yet you still have not reached that magic number. Although your focus may be to lose weight and keep it off, *Put God's Word on Your Weight* was written to help shift your focus from losing weight to receiving your freedom from the weight. Galatians 5:1 teaches, "*It is for freedom that Christ has set us free.*"

God wants us free! And Christ purchased that freedom for us on the cross. This is great news for we know that the bible says, "So if the Son sets you free, you are free indeed. (John 8:36)

FREEDOM! Get that in your spirit; bury it in your heart. It is freedom that we are after! Don't be deceived; it's not the perfect size that we should be going after, it is freedom!

God wanted this book in the earth because of his relentless determination to set us free from *anything* that has us bound. This book, therefore, could have been called **Put God's Word on Your...** debt, sickness, poverty, disease, drug, alcohol, or any other addiction. We can put God's Word on anything that enslaves us by declaring God's Word over it and claiming our freedom forever.

You hold in your hand the total, cutting-edge package to bring closure to the physical, spiritual, and emotional issues associated with your weight. The nuggets herein are grounded in practical truth. They will renew your mind and your body will be transformed in the process. These truths will help expose the root of what is "eating you" and give you strategies to both destroy the root *and* reverse the damage.

Every word that formed a sentence and every sentence that created a paragraph in this book is a testimony to what God will do in the life of *anyone* who comes to the end of themselves and trusts God to lose weight His way.

Whether you have painfully struggled with losing weight for a short period of time or for years, this book will help you understand that the freedom God wants for us is far greater than the pounds that make up our physical body.

God is certainly concerned about our weight because it concerns us, and God promised in Psalm 138:8 to perfect the things that concern us, but God's focus is not limited. He wants us free from ALL the weight that we carry; body weight, mental weight, emotional weight, financial weight, and every other type of weight.

I hope that this book of weight loss declarations and prayers will become a well from which you draw daily and return to again and again to strengthen your inner being. My earnest prayer is that you will come to know and accept God's freedom and let it reign not only in your body but in every area of your life.

Are you ready to *Put God's Word on Your Weight*? Then, let's start at the place where every good work begins…Prayer!

Prayer of Faith for Weight Release
God, You are Awesome! You are the Everlasting Father and You are merciful and almighty.

I admit that I have abused my body with food and I confess that I allowed food to become an idol in my life. Jesus, You bought me with a price and I am sorry for treating my body as if it were my own. I ask You to forgive me and help me overcome my weaknesses concerning food.

Lord, this is the confidence that I have as I approach Your throne: I know that if I ask anything according to Your will, You hear me. Since I know that You hear me always, I am convinced that I have received what I have asked of You. It is Your will for me to be whole and well, so I pray that I will prosper in good health, even as my soul prospers.

I pray that You will cause me to see all the works of the enemy, even if the enemy is me. Teach me to protect my health with Your Word, and help me to lean on You and not on my own understanding and worldly solutions. Holy Spirit, cause me to remember that I am more than a conqueror through Christ who loves me and that all things are possible with Him. I cry out to You El, "The Strong One," who gives me strength. Do not let me throw away my confidence in times of weakness. Deliver me now from the tyranny of weight and erroneous thinking, and as You reveal to me Your plan of escape, help me trust and obey You.

God, help me to speak with the same authority and boldness that You spoke about concerning Your Word in Isaiah 55:11 (NLT), "*It is the same with my word. I send it out, and it always produces fruit. It will accomplish all I want it to, and it will prosper everywhere I send it.*"

So, it shall be with the Word of God that I speak over my body. I send it out, and it will always produce fruit. It will accomplish all I want it to. This is how I put God's Word on my weight.

In Jesus' Name, Amen!

Put God's Word on Your Weight

- Chapter One -

REALLY, GOD?

You should know that writing this book was never my idea. In fact, it took years for me to understand why God picked me, overweight, broken, fearful, failing me, to author a book about overcoming weight.

This book was written to prove that God is vested in setting the captives free. I am a poster child and living proof that God will fight for the freedom given us on Calvary. The freedom to be "free" is a choice that God offers to all who are in any type of bondage. The cross shows us just how willing God is to do *whatever* is necessary to ensure our freedom from sin and death. God so loved the world that He sent Christ, who sacrificed His life for our freedom: freedom from sin, death, eternal damnation, and even weight.

The question is, will you accept that freedom? Will you let God be God in your weight situation? Will you give God the freedom that He needs to take off your weight in the way that *He* wants to do it? Will you finally lay the weight at the foot of the cross, come to the end of your ways and let God handle it? Letting go of the weight is a choice. Deciding to do whatever God tells you is a choice.

As much as I tried to lose weight on my own, I kept coming up short. I tried diet after diet and chased after the latest weight loss plans and infomercial programs. I tell you: I drank juices and lemon tonics; I counted calories, points, and carbs. I ate low fat and high protein. I tried miracle weight loss recipes that included a cabbage soup concoction that still makes me nauseous when I think about it.

I purchased bands, and tummy tuckers; rubber suits and bottle shakers; CDs and DVDs; and I even paid for personal trainers. I ordered weight loss gadgets that I couldn't even figure out how to work—was I supposed to attach it on my waist or put it on my foot? You name it, I've probably tried it! You get the picture! I tell you the truth, I went through trying to take the weight off on my own and it was rough. The only thing that got slim was my bank account.

You would be right to assume that none of those things provided sustainability for my weight loss effort. My thoughts consumed me and convinced me to run to food for comfort. So, there I was—broken, discouraged and feeling defeated once again.

In an attempt to deal with my pain, I would self-medicate by going to a local store to pick up my red, yellow, green and brown pills. You know the ones I'm talking about: the over-the-counter meds called M & M's, which I understood to mean *Medicine & More*. And when I was having a really bad day, I would get the extra strength M & M's, the ones with peanuts.

Oh, the M & M's aren't pain killers? Well, they sure relieved my pain when I popped them. Yep, I started working on them right away, and I felt good for the two seconds it took for them to melt in my mouth. Shortly after taking several doses of my self-prescribed meds though, I felt guilty and spent the remainder of the day beating myself up and feeling physically and emotionally sick. It got pretty ugly at times.

That vicious cycle of eating for comfort and feeling horrible afterward seemed to have no end and no relief was in sight. I had no clue how deeply rooted my eating issues were until Holy Spirit revealed them to me. I was eating in a gluttonous way, and gluttony is a sin. The greater revelation here is this: my eating habits had turned sinful and sin is a spiritual problem. Holy Spirit helped me realize that I did not have the capacity to deal with my weight in the natural because it was not a natural problem. It was a sin problem. We can never deal with sin on our own! It is Christ who deals with our sin. He handled every past and future sin once and for all at Calvary.

Sin has far-reaching effects; it will cause us to love what we should not love and hate what we should not hate. Gluttony turned me against myself. I remember one day being in a dressing room at a shop that specialized in plus sized women's clothing. As I looked in the 3-way mirror, I began to pick myself apart. With tear-filled eyes, I criticized everything I saw in the mirror. It wasn't that I disliked the clothes or how they looked on me; it was *me* that I didn't like! As I stood before the mirror in disgust, I condemned myself for not being able to control my weight. I began to speak word curses over my body and the 3-way mirror agreed and cursed me. Sadly, I believed every single word that was said.

One morning during one of my weekly weigh-ins, I openly wept after seeing the number on the scale. I stepped on and off the scale several times, hoping the number would magically decrease. I began to go at it with myself, again. Saddened by this routine ordeal, I cried out to God as I had so many times in the past and stood on the scale until the numbers faded away. I was broken with no seeming way of escape, but God shined His light on me.

It was as though God was waiting for me to pour out my complaint one more time. He interrupted my pity party with a gentle whisper saying, "*In order for you to lose weight, you need to say something. Speak to the mountain of weight; say something to it that will cause it to move.*" Hum, I thought to myself, I've been struggling to lose fifty pounds for what seems like fifty years, and you're saying to use my lips to get rid of my hips? God ignored that flippant thought and continued speaking; "*If you want to be free, I want you to write a book. This is how you'll overcome this bondage and help others overcome.*" I said, "Lord, you want *me* to write a book? Me. Really, God, that's your plan? I *need* a book!" I chuckled to myself at the thought of my victory coming this way. But God wasn't laughing.

The thought of God picking me for this daunting task was just unimaginable; I was thinking, "God, you do know this is me, right? I'm the one who is just a potato chip away from being crowned the Queen of Lays. Me, God, you want me to write a book? I am totally unqualified. I'm not an author, God." I reminded God that I was a size 18 Women's, not even a regular size 18. I reminded God that I had failed at losing weight a gazillion times. I reminded Him that I had cheated on every diet and never met a cookie that I didn't like. I told God, "I don't know how to write a book, and if I did, I wouldn't have the time or money to do it." I went on and on. I was in full blown denial and frustrated that God was using this as my way of escape.

As you can see, God was neither moved nor impressed by my response or excuses, and He wasn't taking no for an answer. Right then, I knew exactly how Moses felt as he tried to convince God to send someone more qualified to set His people free. I felt like this project would be like the Israelites making bricks without straw when they labored in Egypt. The thought of writing a book seemed impossible to me; however, God did *not* change His mind about Moses' assignment, and He didn't change His mind about mine. Yes, God picked me, overweight, miserable, unqualified, broken me to come along side of Him and open the prison doors for those burdened by weight. This assignment was tied to my own deliverance and I was terrified.

God wanted to bring me out His way, and what I now realize is that God's way to freedom is likely to be the most improbable path. But at the end of the day, He proves that His way is the only guaranteed way of escape.

As I began this journey, I did a lot of thinking about Moses as the Holy Spirit reminded me of the dialogue between God and Moses in Exodus 3:9-10, "*The Lord said, "I have indeed seen the misery of my people in Egypt. I have heard them crying out because of their slave drivers, and I am concerned about their suffering. And now the cry of the Israelites has reached me, and I have seen the way the Egyptians are oppressing them. So now, go. I am sending you to Pharaoh to bring my people the Israelites out of Egypt."*

I was feeling more and more like Moses. I have heard and read that story many times over my lifetime, but I wept when I put myself in it. I still weep sometimes when I think that God chose me to do something with Him that would set people free. I still felt unqualified, but I realized that being unqualified put me in some pretty good company seeing how God used people who were also unqualified to do His Work. There was Moses the Murderer; Jacob the Liar; David the Womanizer; Peter who denied Christ; Paul who killed Christians; and of course Abraham, who tried to help God expedite the birth of the child God promised; whose name is at the *top* of the list in Hebrews 11 Faith Hall of Fame.

Here is the irony of all of this: God sets people apart like me, the most unprepared, unqualified, unlikely, and unworthy characters, to accomplish what He wants to get done in the earth. God looks for availability not capability and makes His strength perfect in our weakness. Not one of those unqualified biblical people that I mentioned could boast. And neither can we boast about anything except God working through us and in us. Look at how scripture explains this;

1 Corinthians 1:27 (NIV) says, *"But God chose what is foolish in the world to shame the wise; God chose what is weak in the world to shame the strong…"* So God chose weak me, foolish me, the one who thought that I could handle my weight crisis on my own. Our God is shaming those strong, worldly, "do-it-our-way," cookie cutter methodologies with the Power of His Word.

Being unqualified to write this book made me qualified! What has God qualified you to step out and do? In those biblical stories of the ordinary folks God used, all were totally unqualified for the extraordinary assignments to join God in His work – pretty much everyone except for the Lord, Jesus Christ. I never thought God could use me to help others sit at the weight Overcomer's table. My "Really God" question was prompted by amazement, a bit of disbelief and sarcasm; much like Abraham who fell on his face and laughed to himself when God told him that he and his 99-year-old wife were going to have a son and that kings would come from her (paraphrased from Genesis 17:15-17 RSV), yet it happened just like God said.

Here's the final point: God may be calling you to join Him in something that He wants *you* to do, and your response may be "Really God?" You may respond to God's call in that way because you failed in the past, or because you feel unprepared, unqualified or just plain scared. No matter the case, one thing is for sure: if you open your heart to the will of God, the Holy Spirit will open your eyes so that you may see what God has placed inside of you to complete His task.

God will empower you to both begin *and* finish what you were created to do. Then the "Really God?" with the question mark at the end will become "Really God!" with an exclamation point to follow the signs and wonders that God will show you in the beautiful realm of obedience.

Put God's Word on It
Declaration of Faith

God, You are awesome in all of Your ways! Thank You for choosing me to do something great for Your kingdom. Help me Holy Spirit to respond to God's call and to join Him in His great work. I choose not to lean to my own understanding, and I make every effort to acknowledge God in all of my ways. Lord, help me to remember that Your ways and thoughts are greater than mine. I choose to follow the Holy Spirit and do whatever He tells me to do during my weight loss journey and beyond. God, I know that it is You alone who will take me to the other side of my weight. I praise You, for You are faithful. In Jesus's Name, Amen

- Chapter Two -

GOD ALONE

As you begin this journey, please don't consider this your battle; we've thought that way and fought like that long enough. This battle is the Lord's. Ours is to fight the "good fight of faith." It will take faith in God's victorious hand to stay focused on what God alone can do. Open your heart to God's truth about His power and you will experience God's truth about victory. It is *God alone* Who secures victory for us.

Have faith in God! This was Jesus' response to Peter after he saw the withered fig tree that Jesus had cursed. (Matthew 11:22 NIV) Faith in God and in His Word is where the weight release begins. You can lose weight and keep it off if you believe you can! When you come to the crossroad where faith intersects with doubt, it is the Word of God that directs the traffic of your mind and steers you in the pathway of victory.

We must trust that God's Word will cause us to overcome our issue with food. It is critical for us to understand that it is not God *and* something else. It is not God *and* the latest diet trends or God *and* a rigorous exercise program; although these things are beneficial, they play a very small part in freeing us from the food death trap set by the enemy.

Only God can show us the way to lasting victory over the weight. He alone has the way of escape because He knows how we got there. God is familiar with the condition of your heart and the falsehood in your mind. It is God who mends what is broken within us and breaks what has a hold on us. It is God's Word that restores our soul and resets our emotions, and we must trust in Him alone to release us from every weight that binds us, including sin.

Yes, the "s" word, sin, must be mentioned because the way we eat may be influenced by sin. It is God alone who deals with sin, and His grace and mercy are sufficient to handle it. We will talk more about sinful eating later in the book; for now, I want to offer a special invitation.

The only way that we have access to God and to His amazing grace and power is to experience Him through Jesus Christ. Jesus must be Lord over every area of our lives; mind, soul, and body. Christ offers every believer victory and a seat at the Overcomer's table. In Him, we have access to return to that table again and again for strength and power during our walk on the earth.

Salvation is the first step to yielding to God's purpose and process for our lives. God cares about everything that we care about including the release of excess weight. Holy Spirit (the third Person of the Trinity) is our Spiritual guide and personal trainer. His work is to help us, empower us, intercede for us, and to reveal God's strategies to give us victory in every area of our lives. Holy Spirit is also the One who reveals the character of Christ to us as a model. As the revealer of truth, Holy Spirit will reveal you to you. This includes the root of your behavior, temperament, choices, inhibitions and other human responses. Praise God, for the revelation and truth that Holy Spirit so gently shows us as He helps us work through our stuff. This work is God's alone, and His work is comprehensive. It exposes seeds of deception, doubt, fear, and the deep-rooted issues of generational curses that shape the baggage that we carry.

God, in His complete love and sympathy for our weaknesses, does not offer revelation without restoration. God has not left it up to us to figure things out for ourselves after He shows us our frailty. Neither does God expect us to figure out how to get out of any type of bondage. If man could have figured that out, then there would have been no need for Christ and the work of the cross. Freedom is ours because of God alone; however, God requires our participation in maintaining the freedom that was so graciously purchased for us at Calvary. At the core of our freedom is the power to choose.

Hear God's words in Deuteronomy 30:19 (NLT) to the children of Israel, *"Today I have given you the choice between life and death, between blessings and curses. Now I call on heaven and earth to witness the choice you make. Oh, that you would choose life so that you and your descendants might live."* Do you see that? In this scripture, whose decision was it to choose life or death? It was theirs! God did not make that decision for them; He put it before his people to decide.

This fact is even true of the salvation that God offers to everyone. A decision must be made by the individual to take God's offer of eternal life. As much as God loves us, and as much as He wants us to be free from every yoke of bondage, including excess body weight, God leaves the decision for us to exercise the right that He gave us to choose.

Job 22:28 (NIV) says, *"What you decide on will be done, and light will shine on your ways."* So, the first step in the God-size process to release excess body weight or any weight for that matter is to make a "decision." For example, you may want to start with a decision to let God show you how to take off the weight. Remember, God's ways are not your ways. This decision will set the foundation for faith to go to work. Let's take God's promise in Job 22:28 and make it into this declaration of faith. "What I decide on *will* be done concerning my weight, and the light of God will shine on my ways." Remember, victory or failure begins with a single choice.

What you decide to do or not do from this point comes down to what you believe. It is about the choice to believe and to commit to doing what you believe, by faith. This choice determines what you believe about the power of God. If you attend to God's Word, meditating on it and declaring it over your weight, God will release a weight loss anointing upon you that will remove the burden of weight and destroy the yoke of bondage to it. This is promised in Isaiah 10:27 (KJV), *"And it shall come to pass in that day, that his burden shall be taken away from off thy shoulder, and his yoke from off thy neck, and the yoke shall be destroyed because of the anointing."* What is the anointing? It is the burden removing, yoke destroying power of God. The anointing destroys any weight that gets in the way of your freedom and God's best for your life.

I pray that you will be fully persuaded by the power of God's written Word, believing and declaring what God has prophesied about you. He saw *you* in the "shall be." God prophesied that you and I were more than conquerors through Christ Who loves us, and that we can do all things through Christ Who gives us strength. Do You believe that?

We must believe the words that God has spoken over us. If you have struggled to lose weight for a long period of time like I have, you may have doubts that you ever will. You probably have asked yourself repeatedly: will I ever lose this weight? This doubting and questioning perpetuates unbelief. There is an impending danger at hand when unbelief takes residence in our hearts and minds. Unbelief is a thief that comes to rob us of the hope that we so desperately need to overcome the weight.

We see unbelief at work in the book of Exodus (Chapters 16 and 17). The Israelites struggled with unbelief and did not believe that God would provide for them and take them safely to the Promised Land. It was not God Who kept them from the great future He had promised them; it was their unbelief.

God would have taken each of His chosen people to the other side of the bondage they had experienced if they had only trusted and believed that He would do it. Even though God rolled back the waters of the Red Sea and the Israelites walked on dry solid ground, they still did not trust God in their wilderness experience.

How many times has God made a way for us to get out of a tough spot, protecting us from evil, sending manna from heaven when our cabinets were bare, saving us from dangers seen and unseen — even from ourselves? The God that drowned Pharaoh's army and parted the Red Sea is the same God that will keep you from eating that second bag of Cheetos. Seriously, the truth is that we can never do for ourselves what God alone can do. Our only hope lies in Him; without God, we have no real power. It would, therefore, be safe to say that any power outside that which is given to us by Christ is generic; God's power is the brand.

Choose to believe God and trust in the power of His might. We must become fully persuaded and aggressively take hold of the faith of our forefather Abraham. Let's look at Romans 4:18-21 (NIV) *"Against all hope, Abraham in hope <u>believed</u> and so became the father of many nations, just as it had been said to him, 'So shall your offspring be.' <u>Without weakening in his faith</u>, he faced the fact that his body was as good as dead—since he was about a hundred years old—and that Sarah's womb was also dead. Yet he <u>did not waver through unbelief</u> regarding the promise of God, but was <u>strengthened in his faith</u> and gave glory to God, <u>being fully persuaded</u> that God had the <u>power</u> to do what he had promised."*

Wow! There it is, at work: faith and belief in what God alone can do. Abraham had to *believe* what God said in order to *receive* what God said. He saw himself as the Father of many nations. Can you see yourself losing weight and keeping it off? Put God's Word to work on your weight and tap into the same power that gave Abraham a son at one hundred years old. Abraham was a believer. He believed in God.

We will be free from weight forever and take a seat at the Overcomer's table that God prepares for us in the presence of our enemy, the devil. If you believe in Christ, the Son of God, you have been given the power to speak to the mountain of weight and move it. It is God alone who gives us the power to do so. But remember, God is always going to do things His way, and His way to freedom and deliverance is through Christ Jesus. Remember I told you earlier that I wanted to offer a special invitation?

So, do you have a place at the Overcomer's table? God extends an open invitation to everyone. There is a place for you if you have not yet accepted the invitation; may I offer this life changing opportunity to you now? Just say this simple prayer: "Jesus, I believe that you are Lord and I believe in my heart that God raised you from the dead. Forgive my sins, come into my life and help me live for you. Thank you for saving me. Amen."

According to Romans 12:9-10 (NIV), *"If you confess with your mouth Jesus as Lord and believe in your heart that God raised Him from the dead, you will be saved; for with the heart a person believes, resulting in righteousness, and with the mouth he confesses, resulting in salvation."*

God made it just that simple for us. Welcome to the family of faith! It is God alone, Who saves us!

- Chapter Three -

COUNTING LOSSES

Although I never really saw any lasting weight loss results year after year, I did have some significant losses in this grueling battle. I lost time. I lost money. I lost sleep. I lost energy for the fight. And many times, I lost the hope of ever getting a real shot at victory over my weight.

Often as victory eludes us, we slowly fade into the familiarity of failure, accepting it as normal, thus becoming content with it. It is in that place where we grow tired of fighting and consider staying down on the mat, merely listening to the referee count us out. We should use that time of failure to remember the promises of God and trust the word of God to get up. I was on the mat many times, and have lost many fights trying to get us up and lose weight without God's help. Focusing only on the scale and not looking to God caused me to lose much more than my weight loss battle.

Holy Spirit revealed that I had lost a lot more than my fight to get slimmer. I had lost something much more valuable than the inches I wanted off my waist. Somewhere between the mirror, the scale, and the lies of the devil, I had lost some valuable parts of myself. Precious bits and pieces of my worth were whittled away as I kept a close watch on the scale. When I took inventory of myself, I realized that my joy was gone, and my peace had left with it. I was perpetually standing before a three-way mirror that constantly reminded me that I had failed at the one thing that I wanted so badly; to lose weight, and keep it off.

I felt like I was a prisoner in my own body; in fact, I was. I was so distracted by my weight that I lost years of loving myself and enjoying the person that made me…me. I became a watered-down version of myself that I hated. I had my smile but had lost the life behind it. I knew what to do but had lost the zeal with which to do it. I was a prisoner in my own body, a prisoner to the plate with no real freedom in sight.

There are scores of people in plate prison and many of us are in the body of Christ. Christians love God *and* we love food. The bible speaks of having two masters in Matthew 6:24 (RSV), *"No one can serve two masters; for either he will hate the one and love the other, or he will be devoted to the one and despise the other. You cannot serve God and mammon."* This passage is speaking within the biblical context of riches, money, and material possessions; however, I'd like to submit to you that each of them is related to greed. In the case of food, that greed is gluttony.

I believe the Word is true about loving one master and despising the other. I considered this word to be the Holy Spirit revealing truth to me about my allegiance to food. I had pledged allegiance to the plate which kept me from giving God my whole heart. So, I hated that plate master; I hated the control that my precious plate had over me, but I still served it well and enjoyed sinful eating. I knew that I loved God and that I wanted Him to have all my heart, but I was unable to give it to Him on my own. I paid big time for my relationship with food, food that had neither the capacity nor power to satisfy my hungry soul. Only God can fill an empty soul.

The Lord showed me that both believers and non-believers alike use food to satisfy the hunger pains of the soul. We eat to find peace and temporary joy in our relationship with food. Food is relational. We can see that eating together is a big deal in families as well as in the church. Food has always been a part of church culture. We see Jesus and other people throughout the bible having fellowship and breaking bread together. There is a beautiful illustration of this at the Last Supper with Jesus having His final meal with those whom He loved and walked with during His ministry.

Unfortunately, the beautiful custom of mealtime fellowship that is intended to bring us closer together has been perverted and used by the enemy to deteriorate our bodies, our families and the body of Christ. Satan did the old bait and switch on us, so to speak, trying to use the very food that God created to sustain the body to destroy it. Food is one of those legal things in which a believer may continue to partake after salvation. Just think about the post-salvation process of sanctification and what that looks like when we surrender all to God; we don't smoke anymore, we quit drinking, we give up sleeping around and social drug use. So, what's left? Food. And while it is legal and *a necessity*, it is one of the greatest weapons that the devil uses against us. We need to let God deliver us from sinful eating like he did all that other stuff. He is able!

It is absolutely critical to our wellbeing and to the protection of our health that we not only consider the loss here, but that we consider what Satan is trying to gain. He has perverted our relationship with food and sat it on a throne, misappropriating its function. Just look at how we have allowed food to take center stage at our church gatherings and the type of food being served; fried chicken and fish, fat-filled sides and desserts.

We even use food as bait to get people out for a church event or service; we have breakfast events to get people out to pray in the morning, and we sell fried fish dinners, candy and cookies to fund Kingdom business. Sure, we celebrate Christmas and Christ's resurrection, baptisms, confirmations and other sacred events, but food is the main headliner. Unfortunately, the meals have become an even larger draw than the meaning behind these celebrations.

Eating has become synonymous with many of our church activities, and Satan, our cunning enemy, has caught us sleeping at the table while gluttony crept into the church. Count the cost! Obesity is running rampant from the pulpits to the pews. I pray that you won't take offense because I'm talking about sinful eating – gluttony. Satan would love for you to be offended by this so that you can remain blind to his tricks.

God does not want us to be ignorant to the crafty tricks of the enemy. We must remember that over indulgence in food *is* gluttony. Gluttony is the seed sin that gives life to other sins like idolatry, where food becomes a god, the other master of which I spoke of earlier. We must open our eyes and see the ravishing effect that out of control eating has on the body and soul. People are paying a very high price for an early grave, including believers.

God opened my eyes to see how the devil was using food to steal, kill and destroy Christ's body, the Church. I was led to do some simple research on the issue. I began by looking at church services and other religious programs on television. It was astonishing to see how many preachers, teachers, choir and church members of the Body of Christ were overweight, and some were extremely obese. It is one of those things that we see all the time but do not *really* see. I even saw it in my own church.

We see obese people of all races, ages and gender so much that it is normal to look right past the problem. But God wants us to take notice and truly see this life threating issue for what it really is: Death by the fork! The Holy Spirit wants to reveal to us the reality of unrestrained, out of control eating so that He can help us escape it and live whole. One may never see the word "gluttony" written as the cause of death on a death certificate, but in actuality, "no restraint at the table" is the underlying cause of many deaths.

Unfortunately, heart disease, high blood pressure, diabetes and cancer are common place in our culture and in our churches. Our prayer lists are filled with dear saints whose health is deteriorating because of eating disorders.

Let me pause right here to say that there is *"NOW NO condemnation for those who are in Christ Jesus."* (Romans 8:1). Please hear my heart on this: I am not pointing a convicting finger nor am I railing on my church family, and I am certainly not trying to cast some sense of shame or offend anyone. No, I have dealt with the pain of shame and rejection myself for far too long to do that. I am not judging; I am grieving! I am grieving for the quality of life that has been stolen by eating sickness. I am grieving for the people and their families who have died prematurely because of a lack of restraint.

The bottom line is, we are being fooled into thinking we're okay because others around us look like us, eat like and think like us; meanwhile, our children and teens are following in our footsteps, suffering from obesity and diabetes, which are fast-growing health epidemics in the United States. Let's count the cost! People are dying because of food-related illnesses.

Regrettably, obesity has been accepted as the "norm" in this country. We have manufacturers making clothes larger and larger; dishes are bigger because people want their meals super-sized. Statistics show that casket companies have a greater demand for oversized caskets, and the cemeteries are doubling the price for oversize graves.

In support of the world's way of doing things that are not in alignment with God's ways, there is a movement that promotes accepting obesity as a way of life. That erroneous pattern of thinking is somehow being endorsed as "acceptance" of one's size without accountability for protecting one's health. This is a trick that has no treat for there is absolutely nothing positive about having body parts replaced or chemotherapy, dialysis, or taking a hundred medications that cause you to have to take two hundred and fifty more because of their side-effects.

If I sound angry or upset, it's because I am! It is painful to see people, especially God's people being fooled by the enemy and duped into thinking that we can eat our way through life and still be okay. It's a lie! It is not okay to eat ourselves to death!

We must constantly remind ourselves that food is a physiological need that was never intended to be a daily buffet. Overeating and choosing to eat foods that we know are detrimental to our health is a very slippery slope that can indeed lead to gluttony and food idolatry. Let me also take a moment to add that eating in a way that becomes sinful it is not just done by those who are overweight; there are skinny gluttons, which is a sure indication that no one is exempt from sinful eating. The devil ain't choosy.

We must all pray for ourselves and others whose minds have been misled by stinking thinking. We must pray for ourselves and others who have been afflicted by sickness and disease. It should grieve us to see God's beloved children in line waiting for kidneys and heart transplants and needing to have hips and knees replaced. Although God has given man the technology and knowledge to perform these surgical procedures, I don't believe that it was ever God's intention to have our body parts replaced because they have been damaged by the weight we carry. That is *not* God's best for us.

I'm glad that God would not allow me to grieve in silence. He made me tell the truth that He showed me about the attack on the church, Christ's precious Bride. I have been given the mission to expose the enemy and help open eyes to how easily we are persuaded to partake in the demise of our health. Your mission, should you decide to accept it, is to get before God and let Holy Spirit provide you with the understanding needed to be forever free from the bondage of sinful eating and the weight it carries.

God wants you to know that you are not alone and that He has a good plan for you to be healed inside and out. God did it for me and He will do that for you. My weight was a dark shadow that kept me torn up inside for years. Eating was the fig leaf that I used to cover my shame and self-hatred. God has undone my shame and I am no longer hiding; He has given me beauty for ashes and taught me to have a healthy love for myself. The Holy Spirit did that by opening my eyes to see the depth of God's love for me. Yes, Jesus loves me; Yes, Jesus loves you; Yes, Jesus loves us, for the bible tells me so.

Tears are gracing my face as I type these words because I am free to love myself now without conditions, all because of God's love that has been shed abroad in my heart for "me." My heart is bare before you. I am telling you the truth: I was so messed up inside and broken for so long, and I learned to hide it so well…but God brought me out of hiding and into the openness of His love.

God wants you to know that He loves you so much, and He cares about your weight and all your other heartaches. Although I have not lost all the weight that I want to lose at this time, I have lost the heaviness in my heart about it. Actually, I didn't lose that heaviness; I know exactly where it is: I gave it to God and Christ took it away. Christ cut our losses on the cross and prepared a way of escape from the weight that so easily besets us, including the excessive weight that we carry in our hearts. No matter what it is Christ is willing to take it. Give it to him today.

If overindulging in food is sin, and it is, then it was never meant for us to handle it. In fact, we cannot handle any sin on our own. Sin was dealt with on the cross, and it was there that Christ took care of it once and for us all. We can choose to let Christ handle our struggle with food or we can continue in our own effort, which has no power for deliverance.

Throughout history, from the fall of man until today, we have entertained the cunning suggestions of a very savvy enemy. The power of evil suggestion began in the Garden of Eden when Satan asked Eve, "Did God really say…?" That question raised the curiosity that created a desire for something other than God's best and ushered mankind into a state of works and hard labor. But God has given us the power to choose good over evil, and we can say no to the invitation to partake in the banquet of an early grave.

God counted the losses created by sin, and He took the initiative to transfer us out of darkness into His marvelous light by sending His Son to rescue us. It was God's love for us that impelled Christ to pay a ransom for us. He paid a tremendous price to free us from the works of the enemy and from our own works. This precious freedom cost Jesus His life, and He freely laid it down and lifted the grace that brings us home to the Father, to His Eternal Kingdom where we will enjoy Him forever.

All we must do is receive the sacrificial love of Christ. As believers we are supposed to be operating in the kingdom of acceptance and not works. When we accepted Christ, we were positioned to receive His love, power, peace, joy and all the other free benefits that came with salvation. We don't have to work to lose weight; we only need to receive the finished work of the cross.

I lost so much time "working" on my weight. The more I thought I had to work it out, the further I got from the grace I needed to lose weight and keep it off. It is God's grace – His desire to bless us although we don't deserve it. Let God handle the weight with His grace and favor. He is waiting on you to ask Him for help. Decide right now to let God's grace take it from here and wait for Him to give you the next step.

We must open our eyes to what God shows us and not be deceived into thinking that we're okay and that our eating habits are exempt from sin. Put your plate on trial and let the Holy Spirit reveal to you if you are eating in a sinful, gluttonous way. He is our Heavenly Counselor who will speak the truth to us in love, without judging or condemnation.

When we accept the counsel of Holy Spirit we should expect Him to expose every evil suggestion that allows sin to creep into our eating behaviors and when He does reveal them, do something that God loves…Repent! You will be forgiven *and* transformed.

Put God's Word on It
Declaration of Faith

God, I receive Your grace and love. Forgive me if I have sinned against you in my eating, and help me to turn away from gluttony. I trust in the way of escape that Christ has prepared for me to lose weight, and I do not lean to my own understanding. Holy Spirit, help me trust Your counsel and follow Your guidance. Empower me to eat in a way that will bring glory to God in my body. Thank You God for recovering all that has been lost. In Jesus' Name, Amen.

- Chapter Four -

TRANS FORMED

As we ponder our lives, we may realize that the reactions to both our happy and sad times have somehow involved food. We often find ourselves over eating and/or thinking about food in either situation. True, I have used food to self-soothe in sad times, but I was also at my heaviest weight during some of the happiest times in my life.

Think about it: if we get a big promotion or lose a job, we eat. If we're happy in a relationship or nursing a broken heart, we eat. Whether happy or sad, food always seems to play a significant role in the scenario. Why? Because our thinking gets tied up in our emotions and our emotions, good or bad, bring us back to food for comfort.

Ever had a bad day at work and as soon as you got off, you wanted to go out to dinner? Perhaps you experienced a failed relationship or the loss of a loved one; food is often the comfort used as a replacement for that person's presence. You can probably think of a hundred situations like these; I know that I can. No matter how the thing got started, our thoughts and feelings somehow lead us to pick up the fork.

While our minds have been trained to use food to both soothe our souls and to celebrate happiness and joyous occasions isn't it funny that we seem to punish ourselves for taking advantage of those moments of temporary comfort and rewards? For it is after those indulgences that all the crazy self-bashing begins; our thinking goes haywire and feelings and emotions take over once again.

This behavior is dangerous to our physical, spiritual and emotional well-being. So much is at stake here; we cannot afford to let our unchecked, "bull-in-a-China Shop" thoughts roam freely through our minds. In order to protect our health, we must protect our thinking. There is and has always been a battle for the control of the mind.

Whoever masters the mind, rules the body! Will it be God, a person, the enemy – or a plate? Please understand: losing weight and keeping it off is not *all* about our eating behavior. The way we eat has a lot to do with the way we think and feel.

The battle of the bulge will be won or lost on the battlefield of our minds; the true ground on which we fight for weight control. This battle is not a fight for a particular size; the prize is so much greater than being the perfect size. The real scuffle is for the control of your every thought. It is a battle for the soul, the home of the mind, will, and emotions. The soul is where we make choices and decisions which are driven by thoughts. Thoughts become the birthing place for real situations and circumstances; good, bad or indifferent, everything gets started in the mind.

Because the condition of the mind is so critical, it must be trained to think differently. We must have a different mindset if we are to have a different outcome, even when it comes down to eating right. Think right, eat right. Our thoughts about eating and losing weight must be in alignment with wholeness; this is where God wants to transform us.

I love the translation of Romans 12:2 in the New Living Translation Bible as it offers a choice that speaks to doing our part in God's transformation process: *"Don't copy the behavior and customs of this world but, let God transform you into a new person, by changing the way you think."* Now God certainly does not *need* us to let Him do anything; He is all powerful and sovereign. God has given man the freedom of choice, so the "let" that is spoken of in Romans 12:2

(NLT) is also stated as "<u>be</u> ye transformed" in the King James Version of that same scripture.

Let's break down the meaning of the word transform so that we may comprehend it in a manner that is relative to Romans 12:2.

Trans is defined as "*across,*" "*through,*" "*changing thoroughly,*" or "*on the other side of.*" An example of using *trans* as a prefix is "transport" which is *the act of carrying something from one place to another*.

Now let's look at the word "***form***." While there are many meanings of the word *form*, the context in which I am using it is defined as *a person's mood and state of health*. By the Power of God, we can be changed thoroughly and transported to the other side of our weight – from our old unhealthy ways of thinking, feeling, and eating – to a state of health and wholeness.

We can be **<u>trans</u>** <u>*formed*</u> *by the renewing of your mind*. God puts the definitions of "*trans*" and "*form*" to work as He takes us through the mind-renewal process of weight loss, *changing our thoughts thoroughly –trans – forming* our emotions and reshaping our thinking, disposition, and attitude about eating. So, when we are in Christ Jesus, God transforms us by the renewing of the mind; the old disposition, attitude, and character are changed because we are transformed into the image of Christ and thus possess the mind of Christ.

The physical transformation that we so desperately seek is completely dependent upon our willingness to be transformed, giving God complete control of our lives. That process begins at the point of salvation and is an on-going beautification project that stems from the inside out. God does this marvelous, renewing transfiguration through His Holy Spirit.

Now let's look again at Romans 12:2: "*Let God transform you into a new person, by changing the way you think.*" When God changes the way that we think, the mind of Christ Jesus takes over. Our old way of thinking passes away, and we begin to think a new way. Transformation by the renewal of the mind is not some magical, abracadabra, overnight change. It is a process done through the word of God and it takes diligence on our part to not just read and study God's word, but to also allow the word to read us; to tell us about our how's, when's and whys. This is how the mind gets renewed.

Permanent weight loss will follow the renewal of the mind, for our bodies follow our thoughts.

The weight of God's Word will reframe the erroneous thinking that drives our feelings and emotions toward food and redirect our focus to Christ, our hope of glory.

We must trust God to provide the revelation for our transformation. God will expose the underlying causes of our eating behaviors and reveal the truth. It is in this revealing stage that real transformation begins to happen. As we discover the true source of our eating disorder, God will provide strategies to restore us to wholeness. There is no real transformation without God's revelation, and no total restoration without the weight of God's Word.

As the Word of God transforms and renews the mind, the weight of God's Word will destroy the yoke of bondage to food and other forms of bondage. The strongholds of erroneous thinking are fortresses that protect wrong reasoning and secure oppression. Understanding the nature of these strongholds has helped me to empathize with people who struggle with other types of addiction. I began to see their addiction through eyes of compassion once I realized that overeating was an addiction. The drug addict or alcoholic is no different than the over eater. One person's drug of choice may be a bag of marijuana while someone else's is a bag of chips. Although the addictions may be different, many of the underlying causes stem from some type of physical or emotional trauma and pain.

Real transformation begins with real truth. God wants to reveal the truth about our struggle with weight, so His truth can heal our wounded souls and transform us from the inside out. Here's the truth: food is really not the issue. It is merely a fig leaf used to cover up the painful issues that cause us to eat as we do. An insatiable appetite for food, drugs, sex, alcohol and even shopping is an outward cry to fill the empty wells in our hearts that make the soul sick. Only Christ can fill those empty wells.

God wants to "trans" "form" us. He wants to give us the same mind that is in Christ Jesus and make us into a new person. The question is will you let God do it? Quite honestly, we can't do anything without God's help; even making the decision to let God transform us requires God's support and His Word.

Put God's Word on It
Declaration of Faith

Father-God, I admit that I cannot do a thing without you, so I open my heart to your transforming power, and I am changed from the inside out. I declare that I have the mind of Christ which is renewed by the Word of God. I expect God's transforming Word to produce a harvest of good health by healing my heart and soul. As my mind is renewed, I am physically transformed. Holy Spirit, help me to trust and obey what you instruct me to do. I take each step of this weight loss journey by faith, believing that it is the Father doing the work. God, I thank You for the real transforming power that I have in Christ Jesus. Amen.

- Chapter Five -

THE COACH

It has taken me a long time to understand God's transforming power. After years of struggling, my weight seemed to have taken on a life of its own. Every day was the same: I woke up miserable and went to bed miserable. The more I ate, the more I suffered and the more I suffered, you guessed it, the more I ate. I felt hopeless and helpless.

It wasn't until I opened my heart to God – for real, for real – about my weight that I began to see how much He cared about my suffering. God had always heard my cry and He always wanted to help, but He was waiting for me to come to the end of myself and trust Him to handle my weight. Holy Spirit showed a side of Himself to me that I had not come to know. He was my very own personal trainer and life coach, waiting to help me with my weight. He stepped in when I stepped out. He was waiting for me to accept His help.

Early on during our training sessions, my Holy Spirit Life Coach guided me to God's promise in Isaiah 41:10 (NIV); I read it, and said it, and hid it in my heart until I believed God would help me. I hope you will also believe God and take Him at His word when He says to you: *"So do not fear, for I am with you; do not be dismayed, for I am your God. I will strengthen you and help you. I will uphold you with my righteous right hand."*

I believe that God really wants us to get this promise, so He repeated it two more times in Isaiah 41:13 and 14 saying: *"For I am the Lord, your God, who takes hold of your right hand and says to you Do not fear; I will help you…I myself will help you."*

Stand on Isaiah 41:10-14, and use it to remember where your help comes from. Use the Word to lose weight, to get out of debt, to overcome sickness, to help in your marriage and in any other areas where you need God's help. I have stood on this scripture for years and passed it on to others; it is powerful and comforting.

We must continually pray *and* speak the Word of God to remind us that God's promises are guaranteed by His Word. The Word is how we are strengthened in our soul and how our fears are dispelled. As the Holy Spirit began to expose the lies behind my long suffering and replace them with His truth, do you know what I found out? I found that none of it had to do with my weight. It was the things that were weighing me down emotionally and spiritually that kept me running to food for help.

Holy Spirit revealed to me that it is not what we are eating, smoking, or drinking that cripples us. It is what's eating at our hearts and drinking our joy that causes us to continually self-medicate with food, alcohol, and drugs. These addictions manufacture a false peace that really is no peace at all, for they are not capable of handling our deep-rooted, unresolved issues of bitterness, rejection, and unforgiveness. We use these false aids because they appear to help us, but they are in fact the very leeches that suck the life out of our hope and nurse our pain with more pain.

I found that food was a false god that promised me what could *only* be done by the Holy Spirit. Was the food lying to me? ABSOLUTELY! This brought me to the end of myself and to the realization that I was helpless on my own. I had finally come to the place where I had to choose to let God help me.

I once heard a popular pastor say, *"If you make the choice, God will make the change.*" It was becoming clear that God was the only one who could change me. In fact, I realized that it is not even our responsibility to change ourselves. Our part is to make the choice to *let* God change us and trust the work and grace of the Holy Spirit. We must surrender our will to the Life Coach and be trained to let it all go.

I made the choice and my God made the change. Glory to Jesus! In my training sessions with Holy Spirit, "The Good Life Coach," I felt safe and I gave Him access to my wounded soul. He carefully untangled me from the pain of my past, unpeeling layer after layer of hurt, shame, guilt, condemnation, and rejection. These were the emotional weights that kept me tied to my physical weight. As the Holy Spirit was renewing my mind, He was changing me into a new person. I felt lighter than the weight I was carrying because I was being carried by the Word of God.

God has given us a great "Life Coach," Holy Spirit, who helps us choose a better way, a new way, God's way. Our Divine Coach is an answer to a beautiful prayer request made on our behalf by Jesus.

Jesus put in a prayer request before He checked out of the earth. Here it is in John 14:16 (ESV): "*And I will ask the Father, and he will give you another Helper to be with you forever.*" I tell you, Jesus has so much compassion for us that He asked God to send us help "forever" because He knew that as long as we were on this earth, we were going to need help in order to live as conquerors. Can you say Thank you to Jesus, our High Priest who intercedes for us daily at the right hand of the Father? Jesus prayed to send us our Helper, The Wonderful Counselor, The Life Coach, Who is The Holy Spirit!

As our Helper forever, Holy Spirit is working to ensure that we maintain the freedom for which Christ died. Christ won it on Calvary and finished it there! His love is enough to ensure that we overcome every sin and struggle.

Holy Spirit is the One who reveals the person of Jesus and helps us to understand and receive the love of God. He breathes life into our understanding of the gospel truth. Our Divine Life Coach works on Team Trinity with God, the Father and Jesus, who tells the Holy Spirit how to help us.

We see Jesus explaining this truth to his disciples in John 16:13-14 in the NIV; hear his words: *"But when he, the Spirit of truth, comes, he will guide you into all the truth. He will not speak on his own; he will speak only what he hears, and he will tell you what is yet to come. He will glorify me because it is from me that he will receive what he will make known to you."*

Jesus is on His throne, seated next to the Father in Heaven. God deposited the Holy Spirit within us to help us successfully maneuver through life on earth as children of God. It is Holy Spirit Who helped Jesus during His time on earth. Holy Spirit gets things done according to the will of the Father. Let's go deeper; Holy Spirit, our Supernatural Personal Trainer and Life Coach is the One who strengthened Jesus through the torture that He experienced prior to and during His crucifixion.

We have at our disposal the same power of the Holy Spirit Who also raised Christ from the dead. Now, imagine the Holy Spirit using that *same power* to train, counsel, and raise you from every dead situation in your life, including your weight. I really hope that you grasp who is working with us! When Holy Spirit comes alongside you in your weight loss journey, you have the power to be done with weight forever.

Holy Spirit is our Counselor. The Greek translation for the word counselor is *Paraklétos*: called to one's aide, advisor, and helper. Christian theology uses the word *"paraclete"* which is derived from *Paraklétos*. We see the Paraclete actively at work in Genesis 1:2 when God created the heavens and the earth. It was Holy Spirit Who hovered over the waters waiting to breathe life into every "let there be" spoken out of the mouth of God. Holy Spirit is still actively involved in giving power and life to the Word of God that is spoken by the believer today. Do you understand the power of the Holy Spirit? The *same* Spirit that joined God when He created the heavens and the earth is willing to help create a new you, inside then out! We must recognize and accept the Life Coach that resides in us; Holy Spirit, the third Person of the Holy Trinity is God at work in us. He will help us lose every pound of extra weight carried on the body, in the heart, and the depths of the soul. That is His job. He is our Helper.

This Divine Life Coach uses the Word of God to fortify our inner being, building us up in holy faith, training us to effectively deal with weight control; however, it is important to understand the role of our good Life Coach. God did not send the Holy Spirit to do the work for us; instead, Holy Spirit was sent to empower us to do what He gives us the power to do.

We must trust God's appointed Life Coach, for He is well able to accomplish the will of God through us, causing every weight to be released by the truth of God's Word. Our part in the life coaching process is to trust, listen and obey the counsel of the Holy Spirit for He is our personal trainer.

Let's look at the responsibilities of a personal trainer or life coach: Generally, the trainer will establish a training program specifically to help the client reach their goal. The training includes a commitment by the trainer and by the trainee to work together. They agree to meet on a regular basis and they work on one accord. This is the same process used by our *Supernatural Personal Trainer.* We must meet with our trainer on a regular basis, so that we can receive instruction and guidance.

To hear what Christ has given the Holy Spirit to say to us, we must position ourselves to listen as the Holy Spirit listens. We need to sit quietly and be taught by the Holy Spirit, Who works in tandem with God the Father, and Christ, His Son, to live in the freedom that God has for us. It is in those quiet personal training sessions that our Life Coach reveals God's plans and extends the grace and power needed for us to succeed in those plans.

Although sitting still in quietness may appear to be inactivity, it builds spiritual muscle like exercise does in the natural. When God says in Psalm 46:10, *"Be still and know that I am God,"* it is *not* a suggestion. It is a *commanded strategy* that will allow us to see all that God is and experience His strong power in a personal way.

One of my favorite scriptures is found in Isaiah 30:15 (NLT): *"This is what the Sovereign LORD, the Holy One of Israel, says: "Only in returning to me and resting in me will you be saved. In quietness and confidence is your strength…"* God told the Israelites to return to him and they would find rest, be saved and have confidence and strength. Then God spoke of their rejection of His offer in Isaiah 30:16, *"…but you would have none of it, you said, 'no, we will get our help from Egypt…"*

God is offering us the same rest that He strategically offered to the Israelites. Let's partake in His rest which includes confidence, strength and ceasing from wrestling on our own. We see in Isaiah 30:16 that God's people refused His help; they said they would get their help elsewhere. I can almost hear God saying,"Let me know how that works out for you."

God wants to help us. So would we rather do things our own way, depending on ourselves, some diet, or some other way to freedom from weight instead of resting confidently in God's strength and trusting in His way? God is saying to us, come to me and rest in this place of peace that I have prepared for you in my presence. Will you be like the Israelites and have "none of it" or will you accept the help from God's Life Coach?

When we wait in God's secret place and sit at the feet of the Divine Personal Trainer, we give Holy Spirit the quality time needed to guide us into all truth and rest in God's love. Just a moment in God's presence can change everything.

Here are a few strategies that I believe will help you establish a plan to remain in constant contact with your Divine Life Coach. First, may I ask that you <u>do</u> <u>not</u> take these suggested strategies and create little laws of them, falling into a religious spirit. Satan would love to set this trap to bring you into condemnation. The first time you miss a step, he will use your little law against you to make you give up and quit. Don't fall for that. Instead, use these strategies as stepping stones to help guide your weight loss journey. Tweak them and master them if you need to, but for heaven's sake, don't let them master you!

#1 Make Divine Appointments

Schedule time to get with your Divine Life Coach; important things are scheduled! Be intentional about the time that you plan to spend together. The Holy Spirit is always available; you just need to be. Put your coaching sessions on your calendar and set reminders if you need to like you do for other important appointments. Keeping in constant contact with the Holy Spirit will help prepare you for whatever is ahead. Your Life Coach will download God's plans for your success into your heart. Keep those divine appointments sacred!

#2 Write What You Hear

Make sure that you write down what you hear Holy Spirit telling you. Write down any instructions that are given to you so that you don't forget. Statistics show that people are more likely to do what they have written down. The Bible was written by people whom the Holy Spirit inspired. They were inspired to write what they heard and saw; we are still being trained by what they wrote hundreds of years ago. May I suggest that you use a journal to write what you hear from your Divine Life Coach and refer to the lessons and strategies as needed.

Reflecting will also ensure that you stay on track with the plans that the Coach has established. Things that are written also create vision and focus. Habakkuk 2:3 says to write the vision down and make it plain. Keep the vision before your eyes so that you can run with what you see. In other words, think in pictures and write or type what you think on paper.

#3 Ask for Help

We all need someone to help us be accountable; of course, you have the Holy Spirit to help you, but you will also need help from someone who loves you enough to hold you accountable for protecting your health and who will encourage you to finish what you've started. That person or persons must also be able to hear from the Holy Spirit. They must be gentle like God and able to speak the truth in love without judging or criticizing, which can cause further damage to your tender soul. Choose someone who will pray for you to receive your freedom and encourage you to trust God for your weight release. They are the one(s) who will pray that you will not fail and/or get weary, and they will comfort you if you do.

Don't try to choose someone on your own. May I suggest that you ask Holy Spirit to show you who He has picked out to walk this journey with you? Your Life Coach may select someone you would never have chosen. As you pray for help, God will give you "His plan," but you must make the decision to do *whatever* He tells you to do. Don't forget: God's ways are not like ours.

Put God's Word on It
Declaration of Faith

Jesus, I thank You for praying to the Father to send the Holy Spirit to help me. Holy Spirit, I acknowledge You as my Counselor, Helper, and Personal Life Coach. I acknowledge You as God. I trust You to train me in the way that Jesus would have me to go. I listen for Your voice, and I am empowered to operate in the will of God. I choose to practice the presence of God and to allow You to show me how to lose weight God's way. I receive Your help and take hold of Your counsel. I see myself whole and well as I am more than a conqueror through Jesus Christ who loves me. Thank you, Holy Spirit, for being my Counselor and Good Life Coach. Amen.

- Chapter Six -

THE ALTAR

Time spent in the presence of God will fortify your faith in His ability to take you to the other side of your weight. Just like the muscles in the body are strengthened through exercise, so is our faith. It is by faith that we overcome. Our faith comes by hearing and hearing by the Word of God, His voice, spoken in both the written Word and through the words whispered to our spirit man.

Consistent encounters with God will lead you to a place of sweet surrender. This is the place where you give yourself completely over to God and fully embrace His Perfect Will. You will find yourself in that place over and over again, wanting more of God. Your willingness to surrender all unto God will take you to a very deep place of worship. Developing a hunger for the presence of God will decrease your hunger for everything else, for no other thing can compare to or even come close to the sweet taste of His glory. You will taste and see for yourself that the Lord is good, and His goodness is more than enough!

The sacred place where you meet God in the beauty of His holiness is your altar; the place where God will ask for you. The sacrifice of "you" in worship is gratitude for the sacrifice of Jesus, Who became a living sacrifice one time for all of us. As you offer yourself as a living sacrifice, holy and acceptable to God, you will experience the same power that lifted Christ from the grave. God is waiting to raise you up from the grave of shame, fear, pain and rejection; when you let Him, you will never be the same.

Worshipping God in spirit and in truth requires a sacrifice. In Genesis 4:3-5, we see Abel offering a sacrifice. The Hebrew term for this type of offering is called "*minha*" which, in this context, means a gift or present, for Abel offered God his best; he gave God what was required, and it was pleasing and acceptable to God.

Let's examine part of the story of Cain and Abel in Genesis 4. Genesis 4:3-4 teaches, "*In the course of time Cain brought some of the fruits of the soil as an offering to the LORD. And Abel also brought an offering—fat portions from some of the firstborn of his flock. The LORD looked with favor on Abel and his offering.*"

This very familiar story gives a narrative about Cain becoming angry because God did not look at his offering with favor. God responded to Cain in Genesis 4:6-7 with this: "*Then the LORD said to Cain, Why are you angry? Why is your face downcast? If you do what is right, will you not be accepted? But if you do not do what is right, sin is crouching at your door; it desires to have you, but you must rule over it.*"

Unlike Cain, Abel worshipped God by giving Him his very best offering. We can also worship God by giving back to Him what Jesus paid for in full—every bit of us: body, mind and soul. We run the risk of sin crouching at our door with the desire to consume us if we don't surrender our whole hearts to God. Sin will not stop until it captures our hearts completely as it did with Cain.

The devil tries to imitate God. So, just as God wants our entire being, so does Satan. Fortunately, God will never give up on us. He will continually send the Spirit of Jesus to bring us back home, and just like in the story of the prodigal son, we come to ourselves.

It is not difficult to figure out from the story of Cain and Abel that God only desires the best. It is important to note that God did not reject Cain; he rejected what Cain offered. God wanted the best that

Cain could give Him. God is not looking for perfection, for there is none; He looks for the submission of our best. What does our best look like to God? Jesus tells us in Mark 12:30-31: "'*Love the Lord your God with all your heart and with all your soul and with all your mind and with all your strength.' The second is this: 'Love your neighbor as yourself.' There is no commandment greater than these.*"

Abel gave God his best offering. There is no substitute for the best. God proved this by making Christ a substitute for us at Calvary. Aaron and other priests in the Old Testament were temporary substitutes who built sacrificial altars to atone for sin, but God gave His best in Christ, where the bloody, sacrificial exchange on the cross made us righteous and acceptable to God forever. Again, I say there is no substitute for the best – give God YOUR best self!

The Acceptable Sacrifice
God no longer requires burnt offerings like that of Abel's. If we listen in on David's conversation with God in Psalm 51 of the NLT, we find exactly what God desires from us. David says to God in Psalm 51:17, "*The sacrifice you desire is a broken spirit. You will not reject a broken and repentant heart, O God.*"

God is always pursing us, and He made it very simple for us to remain at the altar of His presence. Here is a promise from God that allows us to keep the altar of our hearts open before Him. 1 John 1:9 says that *if we confess our sin, God will be faithful and just to forgive us and clean us up, again and again…and again* (emphasis added to the scripture). This extension of God's love and grace allows us to seek His face without being condemned and to continue to bask in God's presence.

The Apostle Paul puts it like this in Romans 12:1, *"And so, dear brothers and sisters, I plead with you to give your bodies to God because of all he has done for you. Let them be a living and holy sacrifice--the kind he will find acceptable. This is truly the way to worship him."*

God will accept these earthly bodies as a living sacrifice and receive us at the altar of repentance. He is not looking at the scope of our sin, for sin is no longer our issue; Christ dealt with all sin, past, present and future sin one time, for all on the cross. Instead, God is looking at the depth and sincerity of our repentance. He waits to hear us say, "I'm sorry God, forgive me." And get this: we do not have to wait for God's forgiveness, for He dispenses it while we are still speaking. Our piece is to accept the amazing grace of God's forgiveness and to continue to love God and love people. And yes, loving ourselves *also* falls under these requirements.

Building Altars
We see God's people erecting altars throughout the Old Testament. When people wanted to worship God, they would build an altar to worship and make sacrifices unto the Lord. Do you know that we can still build worship altars to God and offer Him sacrifices? Building altars will help us offer ourselves as living sacrifices to God daily.

Here are a few strategies that will help you build altars from the grocery store to the table:

Begin with the grocery list and make it fun. This is not meant to be some arduous task. Keep it simple; start with a prayer like this: "Holy Spirit, help me to shop for food that will bless my body and not curse it." Prepare to worship in your eating by selecting the best food for *His* temple – your body.

Write a scripture at the top of your grocery list. Keeping God's Word before your eyes will help you build an altar right in the middle of the cookie aisle. This is not to say that you can't *ever* have cookies, but you get my point. God will help you set your mind on food that will edify your body.

Put God's Word on your appetite in the store. If you know you have no control when eating certain foods, then leave them at the store or purchase the mini size. In my house, I know that an *open* bag of potato chips means an *empty* bag for me, so I get the snack size and polish it off with no regrets. The foods that we crave are usually those that we can't control, so pray for wisdom as you approach those sections in the store; you may find that you will not want to bring them home. Remember: don't get into making laws about what you can and cannot eat. "Die-it and "diet laws" are easily broken. You can eat what you want *if* you use wisdom and portion control.

Worship God while you prepare your meals. Put on some worship music while you cook. I have found this to be a great way to keep my mind on eating to protect my health. Pray over your recipes and ingredients, and the Holy Spirit will help you cook. Now if you are not a good cook, then you need to really pray! All kidding aside, you can use times of meal preparation to build an altar in the kitchen and give God praise for providing all your needs.

Set the table for your meals whenever possible. Make an effort to make the table look special. Consider your table more than a place to eat; make it an altar and prepare to worship God, not the food. You may even want to place pretty flowers on the table, even if they are artificial, and marvel at the beauty of nature. Eliminate distractions such as television and electronic gadgets. Distracted eating can easily turn into overeating. Try to eat at least one formal meal daily and concentrate on chewing – not just swallowing your food.

Pray over your food with your eyes open, not closed, and name each thing on your plate that you are asking God to bless. Seeing and naming what's on your plate will help you keep a realistic view of what you are asking God to bless.

This practice is especially important when you dine out. Imagine this prayer: "God, bless this Big Mac, super-sized fries and large soft drink, and let it be nourishment for my body." Okay, really? Food that is unhealthy will produce unhealthy outcomes in the body. While we may pray over food that does not bless the body, it may still sow seeds that produce sickness and disease. Of course, this does not mean that you can't have a burger and fries; it just means that they shouldn't know you by name at the drive-thru.

If we make a deliberate effort to worship from the shopping cart to the meal table, we will not want to put dead food into the temple of the Living God. When you open your heart as an altar for God, He will close every access point through which the enemy attempts to kill, steal and destroy the body.

When we worship God in this manner, we live our lives modeled after Jesus – in true worship. His sacrifice was based on loving the Father and loving people. You may offer yourself as a living sacrifice to God today. Keep His Word before your eyes and hide scriptures in your heart that will keep you at the altar!

Put God's Word on It
Declaration of Faith

Here I am God, offering myself to You as a living sacrifice. I desire to be holy and acceptable in Your sight and to glorify You in my body. I do not lean to my own understanding when I make food choices. I will acknowledge You Lord when I shop for, prepare and eat my meals, and You will direct my path. Teach me to preserve my life and help me to create altars of worship for You along every path that I take. Thank You, God. In Jesus' Name, Amen.

Inspired by Romans 12:1, S Corinthians 6:20 and Proverbs 3:5.

- Chapter Seven -

YOU ARE NOT THE ENEMY

Wherever there is war, there is a real enemy. We should be mindful daily that we have a real adversary, one whose primary focus is our annihilation. This enemy has an army that is calculating and strategically assembled *against* you to kill and destroy you, your family, your dreams, and your purpose...your life!

He is a thief, a liar, a persuader, a mimic, a schemer, a manipulator, a conspirator, and he collaborates with others of his kind to control your mind, will, and emotions. He is your enemy and God's enemy; he is the devil. He is armed and dangerous with one primary weapon that he uses to keep you discouraged, doubting, lethargic, quiet, and fearful; that weapon is your past: your past failures, your past hurts, your past relationships, your past disappointments, your past mistakes, and your past worries.

Now, the only thing that this shrewd enemy can use against you is your past, for he does not know your future; he is not omniscient like our all-knowing God. This enemy only knows what he has already seen and heard. God and God alone knows our past and our future.

Ole Satan may *think* he knows something about your future because he has seen in your past how God has helped you and delivered you, protected and provided for you, rescued you out of his destructive hands time and time again. He has seen God move on your behalf, even when you were unaware that God was working.

It, therefore, stands to reason that this very real enemy has no *real* power over you when the Almighty, all-powerful God is your God. The devil may form a weapon against us, but it shall *not* succeed. Now, that will not dissuade him from the constant attacks to weigh you down with fear and anxiety about your future, but he has no control except that which we give him. God is in control; He holds our very lives in his hands.

When the battle is raging within you, look for the *real* enemy. These words were penned to remind you of this and here is God's word to confirm it:

> *"For our struggle is not against flesh and blood, but against the rulers, against the authorities, against the powers of this dark world and against the spiritual forces of evil in the heavenly realms." Ephesians 6:12 (NIV)*

Understand: you are not fighting against yourself, your own flesh and blood. It is a trick of the enemy to make you think that you are your own enemy, that you are the root of your weight problem. The devil wants to make you think that you are warring against "you," but you are not the enemy!

As long as the adversary can make you think that you are your own foe, he can cause you to speak harshly to yourself, to accuse yourself of the strongholds that he created. If the devil can make you think that this whole weight issue is "all your fault," he can shift your focus from his schemes and make you take ownership for his evil works.

Do not fall for his lies! This war with weight is *not* You vs. You. No, it is a war waged in the heavenly realms. This is a war against God and His people, to kill and destroy us with food. Look at Ephesians 6:12 again. God has already exposed the real enemy and it is not you and me beloved. This war was started in the Garden of Eden by the devil, who wanted to separate us from God, but it was finished by Christ at the cross who reconciled us back to the Father.

You can believe, then, that our struggle with weight is not against our own bodies; it is against Satan and his evil army trying to continually separate us from God. Granted, the devil is the culprit behind every sin; however, we are still held accountable for *our choices* and must deal with consequences like obesity, sickness, and disease. We *must not* allow sin to reign in our mortal bodies and obey its lusts, but remember, we cannot handle sin on our own – nor are we expected to. God dealt with sin and Satan *for* us and Psalm 18:32 says, *"It is God who arms us with strength and makes our way perfect."*

We are strengthened to overcome the sinful nature and God makes our way perfect to deal with the real enemy. When you find yourself fighting against yourself, stop it. Stop judging yourself, for God is the only righteous judge. Stop condemning yourself, for there is NOW, no condemnation if you are in Christ Jesus. Instead, take heed to 1 Peter 5:8 (NLT): *"Stay alert! Watch out for your great enemy, the devil. He prowls around like a roaring lion, looking for someone to devour."*

Clearly, you have an enemy who wants to kill and destroy you, but you need not fear him for the Lord has defeated him and is still fighting for us. He will not devour us. Watch out for him; look for his tactics and traps, but do not look in the mirror: You Are Not the Enemy!

Put the Word of God on It
Declaration of Faith

God thank you for revealing my true enemy. Help me Holy Spirit to discern his activities and attacks that I may be able to stand against them. I believe God's promise in 2 Chronicles 20:17, and I take hold of it: "I will not have to fight this battle. I take up my position, stand firm, and see the deliverance the Lord will give me over weight as I fight the good fight of faith."

- Chapter Eight -

THE WHITE FLAG

While writing this book, I was participating in a book study on humility with my *Empower 4 Change* Ministry Team. We were reading the book "Humility" by Andrew Murray. It wasn't long before I realized that I was in *grace training*. The book study revealed how highly I thought of my own abilities and how much I had excluded God from certain areas in my life. I came to understand that I was prideful, which included my attempts to deal with my weight on my own.

Murray speaks of humility as *"the place of entire dependence upon God."* He explains that pride, then, is *"the loss of humility and is the root of every sin and evil."* [1]

Through that book study, I saw that my weight was weightless to God. As heavy as it was for me to carry, it was nothing for God to handle. He was my overcoming power.

Finally, I understood why the strength and self-control that I attempted to muster up time and time again was futile, never enough to deal with my weight. This revelation was sobering. Sobering. I saw my weakness clearly in the light of God's strength: I was a mere human being created by the Master of all creation –God.

The blinders had been removed and I saw what I needed lying

between my brokenness and my wholeness, covering up even my pride, keeping me from falling further and further into sin. And it had been right there all the time: Grace. God had imparted His grace to me through the humility of Christ Jesus, who made himself nothing, taking on the nature of a servant and modeling for us that the Son of God would do nothing without His Father.

Yes, my lack of humility was the root of my failures, but God's unmerited favor toward me is the essence of love demonstrated by His amazing grace. And that grace is mine and yours.

Andrew Murray has this to say about Jesus' perfect model of humility: "He teaches us where true humility begins and finds its strength – in the knowledge that it is God who works all in all, that our place is to yield to Him in perfect resignation and dependence, in full consent to be and to do nothing of ourselves."[2]

Christ revealed His humility throughout His earthly ministry. Hear His words:

- *"My teaching is not my own."* (John 7:16)
- *"I am not here on my own."* (John 7:28)
- *"I do nothing on my own."* (John 8:28)
- *"I have not come on my own; but he sent me."* (John 8:42)
- *"I tell you the truth, the Son can do nothing by himself."* (John 5:19)
- *"The words I say to you are not my own."* (John 14:10)

Christ was fully man and fully God when He walked the earth, but He acknowledged His need for the Father's help. He depended on God.

When I looked back over my life and examined the times when I felt strongest, pride had taken center stage. Conversely, when I looked at the times that I was completely weak, I could trace God's grace and perfect strength.

That trip down memory lane revealed that I had been operating in pride for a very long time. I began to see how subtle and far reaching pride could be. I think I was grieved the most when I found that pride's tentacles had reached my prayer life. Holy Spirit revealed to me that pride had made its way into my prayers and tainted them. This revelation was crushing; I wanted to be humble.

So how do we get to humility? We must let Christ be our mentor. We see in Him the perfect model of humility, totally submitted to the Father. He left His throne and majesty to become a servant so that God could become Father to us.

Learning about pride and its effects on mankind should bring us to our knees. Any time we attempt to do anything on our own, we give ourselves over to pride, opening the door for the enemy to trample on us. No wonder the Bible tells us that "pride comes before the fall," for surely, we will fall under the weight of our own frailty.

Raise the Flag
It became crystal clear that pride was seated on the throne of many of my successes and failures. It certainly was the reason that every attempt to lose weight on my own had failed. I bought into the lie that my weight was the thorn in my side, but I know now that pride was the thorn.

When God told Paul in 2 Corinthians 12:9-10, *"My grace is sufficient for you and my power is made perfect in weakness,"* Paul replied in verse 10, *"When I am weak, I am strong…"* Paul's statement would appear to be an oxymoron, but it is not.

I believe that Paul realized that God's power was centered in the midst of God's grace and presence. Our weaknesses are magnified when our finite strength proves to be totally insufficient to handle what only God's grace can. If we admit that we are strongest when we are weak, then we raise the white flag in the presence of the all-sufficient God and surrender all unto His immeasurable strength.

It is in accepting our weakness as the foundation for all our success that we can, without reluctance, take rest in that weakness and let it raise us up in God's perfect strength. This is the perfect formula for freedom and stress-free living.

Want to really be free from weight? Then raise your white flag. The white flag is an international symbol that one uses to concede to the power of one who is stronger. This works in the kingdom of God, too. When we raise the proverbial white flag in the presence of Almighty God, we are surrendering to "El," which means *God, the Strong One*. With our hands lifted, we humbly submit to God's sustaining power, saying, "God, your strength is made perfect in my weakness, so I surrender." I found that as soon as I became *strong* enough to be *weak*, God showed Himself stronger, making my victory sure.

Put God's Word on It
Declaration of Faith

Father God, I humble myself before Your mighty hand, and You will lift me up and take my weight off in due season. Jesus, I take Your yoke upon myself so that I may learn from You how to be humble in heart, and find rest for my soul. Holy Spirit, expose pride and remove a haughty spirit from me for it leads to disgrace. Teach me to be humble and let it bring me honor and wisdom. God, I desire to have a heart of humility. Give me the courage to become weak so that I may be strong in You. In Jesus' name I pray, Amen.

Inspired by: 1 Peter 5:6, Matthew 11:29, Proverbs 11:2 and Proverbs 29:23

- Chapter Nine -

SAY SOW

The laws that govern sowing and reaping are not only relative to the world of agriculture. This law works the same and produces the same type of result in the spirit realm. If a farmer plants a watermelon seed in the ground, he is expecting to reap a harvest of watermelon. It would be an unrealistic expectation for someone to sow red pepper seeds and look for a harvest of green peppers. The law of sowing and reaping operates on one principle: you will get out the same thing that you put in, thus supporting the adage, "You reap what you sow." The expected outcome of harvest time is established when the seed is planted in the ground; therefore, you will get what you have sown.

When we look at this principle operating in the spiritual realm, we see it at work with the words that we speak. Words are seeds planted in the ground of outcomes. We see this principle in full effect when God created the earth. God filled the Heavens and the earth with His words. This means that all created matter – sun, moon, light, waters, etc. – was responsive to the words that God used to call them into existence.

From Genesis 1:3 (NIV), we can glean great insight from the way God works the principles of sowing and reaping: *"And God said, 'Let there be light,' and there was light. God saw that the light was good…"* God repeated this successful process over and over in Genesis 1:6, 1:9, 1:11, 1:14, 1:20, and 1:24, and these scriptures give testimony to the power of the spoken word. God stated seven times that what He created was "good." He only used His words to produce the outcome that *He* wanted. God wanted to see light, so He said, "Light, Be." Every word that God spoke went out into the earth with God's power behind it to accomplish His will. Not one word returned without yielding a harvest from the words that God had sown. Everything that God said, God saw! Then God said it was good. God created man after He had prepared everything for him with His spoken word. We were created in God's likeness and image which means we were created to be speaking beings, with the power to create with words just like the Father who created us.

We see the seedtime and harvest principle at work in John 3:16, *"For God so loved the world that he gave his one and only Son, that whoever believes in him shall not perish but have eternal life."*

In other words, God so loved the world that He planted Christ in the earth because He wanted a harvest of righteous people who would not perish but have everlasting life with Him in Heaven.

When Jesus died and was buried, He became the seed that was planted in the ground so that salvation and righteousness would be the harvest available to all who believed in Him.

God planted Jesus, "The Righteous One," and He saw other righteous ones come after Christ, bearing His name: "**Christ**ians." As Christians, we are children of God and our Father has not only given us His image and likeness, but He has also given us access to the power that He used to create this world and everything in it: God gave us His Word.

The Weight of God's Word
God's Word contained within itself everything needed to create the earth and all its contents. That makes God's Word weighty with authoritative power. God speaks highly of His Word in Isaiah 55:11, comparing it to the purpose of the rain and snow that come to the

earth to make things grow. God says, in Isaiah 55:11(NLT), *"It is the same with my word. I send it out, and it always produces fruit. It will accomplish all I want it to, and it will prosper everywhere I send it."* God is telling us in this scripture that His Word will get things done.

Just as God's Word did not return empty handed in Genesis but gave up what God told it to harvest, so shall it be with us when we practice this principle. If we <u>say</u> what God says, we <u>sow</u> into the realm of endless possibilities and reap a harvest of good. I call this "Say Sow": *Saying* the Word, *Sowing* the Word, and *Seeing* the Word manifested, just like God did. That is the "Weight of God's Word" in full demonstration: Word seed producing Word fruit!

May I caution you about the law of "Say Sow"? It works both positively and negatively. You can exercise the Say Sow principle using words that will bring a good or bad harvest. Remember: every seed produces fruit after its own kind. For example, if you speak negatively about yourself saying something like, "I am the biggest one in my family," you are sowing words that will bear fruit that looks like what you said. Low and behold, every family picture will bear out your words; you will be the biggest one, just like you said, because words have the power to produce after their kind. Put God's Word on Your Weight and the Word will reframe your thinking. Our thoughts become the things that shape the words that we say. The wrong words can create a mountain.

Instead of saying things that make the mountains *grow*, say something that will make the mountains *move*. That's what God told me when He commissioned me to write this book. So, let me ask you this: How big is your mountain?

Your mountain, whatever the type or size, is waiting for you to *say* something before it moves. It is waiting for you to be the boss of it and *command* it to move. The words coming out of your mouth *must be* equivalent to the size of your challenge. You may only need to whisper a few words to move a pile of dirt; as a matter of fact, you could probably just kick it out of your way. But a mountain? Let's be serious, you will have to have a big mouth filled with the Word of God to get that thing out of your way. We know how BIG God's Word is, so the question becomes: "How big is your mouth?"

Remember, I told you to let Jesus be your mentor. When Jesus spoke to the fig tree in Mark 11:14, He told that tree that no one would ever eat from it again. We see later in Mark 11:20 that the tree withered and dried up from the root. Let's pick up the story in Mark 11:21-23 (NLT),

> *Peter remembered what Jesus had said to the tree on the previous day and exclaimed, "Look, Rabbi! The fig tree you cursed has withered and died!" Then Jesus said to the disciples, "Have faith in God. I tell you the truth, you can say to this mountain, 'May you be lifted up and thrown into the sea,' and it will happen. But you must really believe it will happen and have no doubt in your heart."*

Jesus gave His disciples a simple, three-step formula to make the "Say Sow" principle work every time:

1. Have faith in God

2. Say something to the mountain

3. Really believe it will happen and have no doubt

So, look at your mountain, which in this case may be your weight. How big is it? How much weight does it carry? I tell you the truth, it is nothing compared to the Weight of God's Word.

Jesus said that, *"You can say to this mountain, may you be lifted up and thrown into the sea and it will happen."*

The *saying so* is our part to do. Fill your mouth with God's big words and your words will become big enough to move mountains. You can take the weight of God's Word, speak to your mountain of weight and it shall be moved by the word of God coming out of your mouth. We can no longer sit passively hoping that the mountain of weight will one day be behind us. We must put God's Word on it and watch it crumble. But remember, we *must* believe and have no doubt that the Word of God can move the mountain.

In the final chapter of this book, I have provided some power-filled declarations of faith and prayers to help you speak to your mountains. The Word of God is big talk, and it is backed up by the *full weight* of His Power. As you say the declarations in faith, the *Weight of God's Word* will move the mountain of weight, sickness and disease, and any other mountains in your life. You must believe that!

Put God's Word on It
Declaration of Faith

God, I thank you for the power to speak to my mountains. I have faith in You and therefore I will say to the mountain of weight, "be removed'; you have no power over me. I control you; you do not control me." God has placed me above my weight and not beneath it, making me the head and not the tail. I am of good cheer because Christ in me has overcome my mountain of weight.

Inspired by: Mark 11:22-24, Deuteronomy 28:13, John 16:33.

- Chapter Ten -

THE WEIGHT IS OVER

Oh, my goodness! If you believe that putting God's Word on your weight will bring you out, the wait is over! Prophesy to yourself: "The Weight is Over." Now you must believe that every Word that comes out of your mouth has the power to remove every unwanted pound. Believe that because it's true.

There is a blessing that accompanies belief. The Bible says in Luke 1:45 (NIV), *"Blessed is she who has believed that the Lord would fulfill his promises to her!"* God has promised to bless us for believing that He has prepared a way of escape for us to lay the weight aside.

Hear the Word of the Lord in Isaiah 62:10, *"Go through, go through the gates, Clear the way for the people; Build up, build up the highway, Remove the stones, lift up a standard over the peoples."* God is commanding His Word to go before us to prepare the way to our victory over weight. Here is how I interpreted what God commanded His Word to do for us in this scripture: *Go through the gates that have kept them from getting to the other side of their weight. Clear the way for them to get to the other side, and build a highway so that they may escape every weight.*

Now, the last part of this scripture is very significant to our victory. It is God's Word building up the highway that takes us to the other side of through, clearing a path for the weight to be over! It is God's Word that removes the stumbling stones that hold us back. We must know without a doubt that God's Word lifts up a standard over us.

That standard represents the banner of God's love that covers us, and it says to every enemy and every weight: Our God is fighting for us. Take cover under God's banner of love and rest assured that He is well able to defeat every foe, remove every burden, and destroy every yoke and bondage.

The weight is over! We have been moved from the battlefield to the Overcomer's table where we have overcome the weight by the blood of the Lamb and the word of Christ's testimony about us. The Lord has said that we are *more* than conquerors! It took some time for me to accept Christ's testimony about me. It took the Spirit of Truth to convince me that I am who God says I am, and that I have overcome my weight, even though the mirror is yet to testify.

Refuse to accept any other testimony, especially those from the devil, the identity thief. Holy Spirit will continue to empower us to respond to the truth about our image in Christ Jesus, and the weight loss victory that has been assured us through Him.

While we wait for the visible results, we must choose to be led by the Holy Spirit during the weight loss process. Let's take hold of God's Word in Romans 8:14-16 (NIV): *"For those who are led by the Spirit of God are the children of God. The Spirit you received does not make you slaves, so that you live in fear again; rather, the Spirit you received brought about your adoption to sonship and by him we cry, 'Abba Father.' The Spirit himself testifies with our spirit that we are God's children."*

We have received the Spirit of God. We are no longer slaves to our appetite. We will not live in fear of never losing weight, always going through, but never making it to the other side. We are not waiting to be free; we are free now! Our weight will catch up to our testimonies.

Jesus handed us our freedom at Calvary. This weight loss battle was

His from the beginning and His victory is ours in the end. So, praise God for the victory *now*; go on and do your dance *now*; clap your hands *now*! Get in the mirror and celebrate *now* as you patiently wait for the harvest that the Weight of God's Word will surely produce. Start thanking God in advance for your weight release. Giving thanks and praising now is a precursor to your victory. Let's thank God right now.

Prayer of Thanksgiving
Thank You, God! I am standing on top of the mountain of weight declaring it to move by the power of Your Word. Thank You, God, for I will have what I say, and I will see the manifestation of Your Word! Lord, I praise You for my victory over weight. Hallelujah Jesus, Glory to Your Name! Thank You for not letting the enemy triumph over me. You have pledged to never leave me or forsake me. Great is Your faithfulness.

Hallelujah Father–God, I will give You a yet praise for hearing me always. Thank You, God, for lifting my head and for causing all my weight loss efforts to work together for my good health. I love You Father, and I thank You for the liberty that You gave me in Your Dear Son. Thank You, God, the Weight is Over! Amen.

Hallelujah, Holy Spirit. Thank You for helping me overcome the weight. You have been my coach and my guide through it all. Thank You for revealing God the Father and Jesus, my Lord in such a personal way to me. Thank you for giving me access to Your power within me. Thank You, Lord for preparing the way for me to get to the other side of my weight.

Thank You, Holy Spirit for transforming me by renewing my mind and for letting me see my beauty. In Jesus' Name, Amen

Put God's Word on It
Declaration of Faith

My struggle with weight is over and my latter days will be greater than the days when weight had a stronghold on me. I seek God's Kingdom and His ways regarding my weight and God will add victory and triumph. I commit to the Lord whatever I do to lose weight and protect my health, and He will establish my plans. The victory belongs to Jesus for with Him all things are possible.

Inspired by: Job 8:7, Matthew 6:33, Proverbs 16:3, Mark 10:27.

- Chapter Eleven -

I BELIEVE; THEREFORE I SPEAK

As we begin to make our Power Declarations and Prayers for Weight Loss, we need to have a good understanding of what we are doing and why we are doing it. Let me put in this disclaimer before we begin:

These declarations are statements of truth inspired by the Word of God and based on His promises. It is important to understand that the declarations are words void of any power, except that which is given them from the Word of God. The words must be activated by faith, belief, and action.

Just as faith without some type of action accompanying it is considered dead, these weight loss declarations, isolated from belief and action, are powerless to accomplish the desired result. Faith in the Word of God is powerful; however, unless faith is acted upon, things will remain the same.

As powerful as the Word of God is, one cannot speak words of truth over the body and expect the weight to fall off without doing some physical work – action – to change eating behaviors and renew the mind. We must put action with faith as faith standing alone is lifeless.

It is action and faith working *together* that brings life to the possible. Faith in God to release us from the bondage of weight needs something tangible to work with to go forth and bring real weight loss results. In other words, you cannot just talk then run to the mirror and expect a change.

We should be careful not to confuse the works of the flesh, *trying to accomplish something without God's grace and power,* with the action required by faith to *join God* in His work to deliver us. Faith in God and in the power produced by His word is an absolute must, and it must be escorted by action.

Look at it like this: God has a work to do and He is faithful to do it. We cannot do God's work, and God will not do ours. So, are you ready to work *with* the Word of God? Okay, let's begin by declaring what we believe!

"Everything is Possible for One Who Believes" Mark 9:23

I believe that all scripture was written under the inspiration of the Holy Spirit; therefore, I believe that the Word of God will not return to Him empty. As God's beloved child, I imitate my Father, and I speak His infallible Word to establish wholeness in my body and mind.

I believe that the Word of God is useful for teaching and training me to overcome the burden of weight by changing the way that I think. I believe that the Word of God makes me perfect and thoroughly furnished for this good work. I believe that I have overcome my weight issues by the blood of the Lamb and by the word of my testimony.

Inspired by 2 Timothy 3:16-17, Romans 12:1-2, Psalm 33:6, 33:9, Revelation 12:11

I am not in a physical war; therefore, the weapons of my warfare in this weight loss battle are not physical, but they are mighty through God to pull down the strongholds of bondage to food, gluttony, temptation, shame, guilt, and low self-worth. I believe that I am not alone; my God is with me, and this is His battle. I take my position and stand on the word of God, believing that the power of God's words spoken out of my mouth will destroy every yoke that has caused me to be overweight. I put the entire Weight of God's Word on my weight loss efforts, knowing that God's Word has the power to renew my mind, transform and reshape my physical body, regulate my emotions, heal my heart, and change my eating behaviors.

Inspired by: 2 Corinthians 10:3-4, and 2 Chronicles 20:17

I believe the Word of God is a seed that will grow into a harvest of good health in my mind and body. I not only expect to lose weight during this experience; I expect to experience God!

Declarations & Prayers for Weight Loss

PUT GOD'S WORD ON YOUR WEIGHT

Using Your Weight Loss Declarations and Prayers
Your weight loss declarations have power, so the more you speak them, the more potent they become. I know how difficult it may be to find time to consistently make all the declarations, but it is beneficial to declare them all, initially. Imagine that you are creating a declaration sandwich (Think: *Scripture –Declarations –Scripture*). Using scriptures with declaration and prayers in this way is so powerful!

Realistically speaking, time may not permit for you to complete all the declarations and prayers at once. May I suggest that you select one or two declarations to cover the areas where you may struggle most or where you are being attacked by the enemy; hit that place hard and put the *Weight of God's Word* on it several times a day.

Don't fall into condemnation if you don't make it through the declarations and prayers every day. That will cause you to feel guilty and keep you from doing any of them. Do what you can consistently, and God will honor that. Ask Holy Spirit to reveal to you the prayers and declarations that you need for the day.

Here is the strategy to help make your declarations and prayers most effective:

- Read the declaration scripture out loud.

- Proclaim the declarations and prayers (don't just say them; pray them, and speak with authority).
- Read the declaration scripture out loud a second time.
- If time permits, go to the next set of declarations.

May I suggest that you take advantage of audio versions of *Put God's Word on Your Weight*. The declarations and prayers are available on CD and in downloadable formats. Make your declarations on the go: in your car, while working out, or while you're at work.

Play your declarations while you are sleeping and let the Word of God move mountains for you through the night. Listening to the declarations and prayers, even when you are unable to speak them, will build your faith in God's Word while you rest. Wherever, whenever, the audio format is a great way to get the declarations/prayers downloaded into your heart and memory.

Remember: faith comes by hearing, and hearing by the Word of God. Your faith for weight loss will be fortified by hearing the Word of God over and over again; then, speaking His Word aloud and making your daily declarations will move the mountain of weight.

Proverbs 4:20-22 (NLT) is a wonderful reminder of a powerful command and promise from the Word of God. *"My child, pay attention to what I say. Listen carefully to my words. Don't lose sight of them. Let them penetrate deep into your heart, for they bring life to those who find them, and healing to their whole body."*

As I declare the Word of God and speak to the mountain of weight, it will move. I believe what I say will happen for me, for the Word of God is powerful and effective. God, my Father, I put You in remembrance of what You said about Your Word in Isaiah 55:11, *"So shall my word be that goes out from my mouth; it shall not return to me empty, but it shall accomplish that which I purpose, and shall succeed in the thing for which I sent it."* God, I believe YOU!

I AM FORGIVEN

> *1 John 1:9 (TLB)*
>
> *But if we confess our sins to him, he can be depended on to forgive us and to cleanse us from every wrong. And it is perfectly proper for God to do this for us because Christ died to wash away our sins.*

Declaration 1: I am Forgiven

Father, when I confess my sins, I can depend on You to forgive and cleanse me. I confess that I have at some point made food a god. I have eaten uncontrollably and excessively. These are sins of idolatry and gluttony, and I repent for eating that way. Forgive me Lord, and thank You, Holy Spirit for helping me turn away from sinful eating. Father, I receive Your forgiveness now!

Declaration 2: I am Forgiven

I have received God's forgiveness. Now I choose to forgive myself. I forgive myself for speaking word curses and condemning my body instead of blessing it. I forgive myself for abusing my body with food and other things. I am free from past mistakes and failures, and I refuse to be crushed by self-pity and condemnation. I receive my own forgiveness now!

I HAVE GRACE

> *2 Corinthians 12:9-10 (NIV)*
>
> *But he said to me, "My grace is sufficient for you, for my power is made perfect in weakness." Therefore I will boast all the more gladly about my weaknesses, so that Christ's power may rest on me.*

Declaration 1: I Have Grace

Father, Your Word says when I am weak, then I am strong. Help me recognize my weaknesses so that Your strength can be made perfect in me. I exchange my perceived strength for Your perfect power. Lord, I have come to the end of my own strength, and I lay it down. Thank You, Jesus, for Your power and strength that rest on me. God, thank you for Your amazing Grace. It is sufficient for me.

> *2 Peter 1:2 (NLT)*
>
> *May God give you more and more grace and peace as you grow in your knowledge of God and Jesus our Lord.*

Declaration 2: I Have Grace

Father, I freely accept the grace that you have given me to lose weight. I am growing in the knowledge of God and Jesus, my Lord. Grace and peace goes before me, keeping me stable and resilient during my weight loss journey. God, Your grace is sufficient.

I HUMBLE MYSELF

> *1 Peter 5:6 (NIV)*
>
> *Humble yourselves, therefore, under God's mighty hand, that he may lift you up in due time.*

Declaration: I Humble Myself

Father, Your word commands me to humble myself under Your mighty hand. I have seen how small I am in the light of Your greatness. Lord, I need You to lift me up and over my weight. Holy Spirit, help me walk in true humility as I lose weight so that I will not fall into pride. Thank You God for Your Mighty hand that lifts me up.

I SUBMIT

Job 22:21 (NLT)

Submit to God, and you will have peace; then things will go well for you.

Declaration: I Submit

Father, I submit my heart to You today. I submit every concern about my weight to God and I claim the peace that He promised. Holy Spirit, help me continually submit my mind, will, and emotions unto the Lord in this weight loss process. God, I thank You for causing things to go well with me in every area of my life.

NO MORE SHAME

Isaiah 61:7 (NLT)

Instead of shame and dishonor, you will enjoy a double share of honor. You will possess a double portion of prosperity in your land, and everlasting joy will be yours.

Declaration 1: No More Shame

Father, I thank You for taking away my shame. Instead of shame and dishonor, I am prospering in God's everlasting joy. I now have a double share of honor for my former shame. God, I praise You for Your Word has taken away my shame.

Psalm 3:3-4 (NIV)

But you, Lord, are a shield around me, my glory, the One who lifts my head high. I call out to the Lord, and he answers me from his holy mountain.

Declaration 2: No More Shame

Thank You God for You have lifted my head high and shielded me from every shame. I am no longer ashamed of my body. I renounce shame, and I release the pain that it has caused me. Thank You, Lord. I called out to You, and You answered me and removed my shame.

> *Psalm 25:1-3 (NIV)*
>
> *In You, Lord my God, I put my trust. I trust in You; do not let me be put to shame, nor let my enemies triumph over me. No one who hopes in You will ever be put to shame...*

Declaration 3: No More Shame

Father, Your Word says that no one who hopes in You will ever be put to shame. God, I trust You and I place my hope in You. My weight can no longer shame me for God is my glory, and He lifts up my head. Thank You Lord for not letting the enemy triumph over me.

I AM A NEW PERSON

> *Romans 12:2 (NLT)*
>
> *Don't copy the behavior and customs of this world, but let God transform you into a new person by changing the way you think. Then you will learn to know God's will for you, which is good and pleasing and perfect.*

Declaration 1: I am a New Person

I have been transformed into a new person. God is changing the way I think about myself and my weight. I am learning God's good, pleasing and perfect will. During my weight loss course, I walk in the newness of my mind and I see my body transformed. Thank You God, for as you renew my mind, I am transformed into a new person.

> *2 Corinthians 5:17)*
>
> *So then, if anyone is in Christ, he is a new creation; what is old has passed away—look, what is new has come!*

Declaration 2: I am a New Person

I am in Christ Jesus and that makes me a new creation. The old person and old thinking has passed away. I embrace the new life that Christ has given me which includes freedom from the weight that I carry. Father, I thank You for making me over. I have a new view of myself; I look and I see that the new person has come!

> *Ephesians 4:22-24 (NIV)*
>
> *You were taught, with regard to your former way of life, to put off your old self, which is being corrupted by its deceitful desires; to be made new in the attitude of your minds; and to put on the new self, created to be like God in true righteousness and holiness.*

Declaration 3: I am a New Person

I have put off my old self and put on the new me created in Christ Jesus. Holy Spirit, help me put away deceitful desires and my former way of thinking and eating. I am made new in the attitude of my mind. Everything about me is brand new! Thank You God that I am a new person in Your true righteousness and holiness.

I AM BEAUTIFUL

> *Isaiah 61:1b-2 (NIV)*
>
> *…He has sent me to bind up the brokenhearted, to*

> *proclaim freedom for the captives and release from darkness for the prisoners, and to proclaim the year of the Lord's favor and the day of vengeance of our God, to comfort all who mourn, and provide for those who grieve in Zion— to bestow on them a crown of beauty instead of ashes, the oil of joy instead of mourning, and a garment of praise instead of a spirit of despair.*

Declaration 1: I Am Beautiful

Father, I thank You for sending Jesus to bind up my broken heart. I receive the freedom that Christ proclaimed over me; I trade His crown of beauty for my ashes. I take hold of Your joy for the mourning that I've done about my weight, and I receive Your garment of praise for the spirit of despair. God, thank You I will soak in Your oil of gladness.

> 1 Peter 3:3-4 (NLT)
>
> *Don't be concerned about the outward beauty of fancy hairstyles, expensive jewelry, or beautiful clothes. You should clothe yourselves instead with the beauty that comes from within, the unfading beauty of a gentle and quiet spirit, which is so precious to God.*

Declaration 2: I Am Beautiful

Holy Spirit, help me to cease from pursuing the beauty defined by the world. I seek the unfading beauty that comes only from Christ. Lord, I do want to look good and feel good, but I also want to *be* good and reflect Your gentle and quiet spirit. Thank You God; I am reflecting your beauty, inwardly and outwardly.

> Psalm 139:14 (MSG)
>
> *Oh yes, you shaped me first inside, then out; you formed me in my mother's womb. I thank you, High God—*

you're breathtaking! Body and soul, I am marvelously made!

Declaration 3: I Am Beautiful

Father, You made me beautiful and marvelous in my mother's womb. Every time I look in the mirror, I declare the breathtaking works of Your hand. God designed me, made me an original: body, soul, and spirit. I am created in the beautiful image of God. Thank You, Daddy, for making me beautiful, just like You.

MY BODY IS A TEMPLE

> *1 Corinthians 6:19-20 (NLT)*
>
> *Don't you realize that your body is the temple of the Holy Spirit, who lives in you and was given to you by God? You do not belong to yourself, for God bought you with a high price. So you must honor God with your body.*

Declaration: My Body is a Temple

Father, Your Word reminds me that my body is Your temple and I do not own it. Holy Spirit, help me appreciate, honor and respect Your dwelling place and keep it holy. I recognize that I am priceless, for I was purchased with the precious blood of the Lamb. Jesus, I thank You for paying such a high price for Your Spirit to reside in me.

MIRROR ~ MIRROR

> *Romans 8:1-2 (NLT)*
>
> *So now there is no condemnation for those who belong to Christ Jesus. And because you belong to him, the power of the life-giving Spirit has freed you from the power of sin that leads to death.*

Declaration 1: Mirror ~ Mirror

There is now no condemnation for me for I am in Christ Jesus. Mirror of shame, you will not cause me to say that I hate myself or to speak horrible word curses over my body. I take back the power that I've given you, and I mute your voice and opinion. Thank You, God, for reflecting Your truth in the mirror. I am not condemned; I am whole.

> *Psalm 139:14 (NIV)*
>
> *I praise you because I am fearfully and wonderfully made; your works are wonderful, I know that full well.*

Declaration 2: Mirror ~ Mirror

Stand before a mirror and make this declaration daily: I Am Beautiful, I Am Strong, I Am Wise, and I Am Loved by God!

I HAVE HELP

> *Proverbs 3:5-12 MSG*
>
> *Trust God from the bottom of your heart; don't try to figure out everything on your own. Listen for God's voice in everything you do, everywhere you go; He's the one who will keep you on track. Don't assume that you know it all. Run to God! Run from evil! Your body will glow with health; your very bones will vibrate with life!*

Declaration: I Have Help

God, I trust You from the bottom of my heart. Thank You for not leaving me alone to figure out how to overcome my weight. Holy Spirit is my helper, and I listen for His voice to keep me on track. I refuse to assume that I know how to lose weight or escape the bondage of sinful eating. So, I run to God! I flee from evil and Holy Spirit directs my path. Thank You, Holy Spirit for being a present and dependable helper.

I AM FOCUSED

Isaiah 26:3 (ISV)

You will keep perfectly peaceful the one whose mind remains focused on you, because he remains in you.

Declaration: I am Focused

Father, I look to You continually to keep me focused, and I am kept in perfect peace about my weight for I remain in You. God, I thank You for helping me keep my mind focused on Your Word. I keep my eyes on You, alone.

I AM CONFIDENT

Philippians 1:6 (NLT)

And I am certain that God, who began the good work within you, will continue his work until it is finally finished on the day when Christ Jesus returns.

Declaration 1: I Am Confident

I am certain that God, Who has begun His good work in my spirit, mind, and body, will continue His work until it is finally finished on the day when Christ returns. My hope is in the hand of the Potter Who will faithfully finish the transformational work that He has started within me. Father, I thank You for Your finished work!

Hebrews 10:35 (NLT)

So do not throw away this confident trust in the Lord.

Remember the great reward it brings you!

Declaration 2: I Am Confident

Father, I hold on firmly to my confidence in You. I have faith in the weight of Your Word and in every promise You have made. I persevere in confidence that You will cause me to win over my weight. Lord, Your Word *will* control my weight; I know that full well. I receive my great reward for trusting You. Thank You, Father; You are my confidence, and my faith in You will not disappoint me.

I CAST MY CARES ON GOD

1 Peter 5:7 (NLT)

Give all your worries and cares to God, for he cares about you.

Declaration 1: I Cast my Cares on God

I cast the worries and cares of losing weight on God for He cares for me. Father, the weight of Your Word can bear my cares, and Your grace is sufficient to handle them. Thank You Lord; I know that You care about me.

Psalm 55:22 (NIV)

Cast your cares on the LORD and he will sustain you; he will never let the righteous be shaken.

Declaration 2: I Cast My Cares on God

Lord, I cast every care that I have regarding my weight on You, and I know that You will sustain me. As I stand on Your Word, I trust that You will *never* let me be shaken by the challenges that I face to lose weight. Father, I thank You for taking care of my cares.

I DO NOT WORRY

Matthew 6:25 (NIV)

"Therefore I tell you, do not worry about your life, what you will eat or drink; or about your body, what you will wear. Is not life more than food, and the body more than clothes?

Declaration: I Do Not Worry

I refuse to worry about my weight, what I will eat or not eat, or how my body looks at this time. My life is so much greater than what is on my plate; therefore, I choose not to be consumed by what I am consuming. My current weight is temporary, so I do not worry about the numbers on the scale. Father, Thank You; You have made me free from worry, doubt, and fear.

I HAVE VICTORY OVER TEMPTATION

1 Corinthians 10:13 (NLT)

The temptations in your life are no different from what others experience. And God is faithful. He will not allow the temptation to be more than you can stand. When you are tempted, he will show you a way out so that you can endure.

Declaration 1: I Have Victory over Temptation

God, You promised that temptation would *not* be allowed to be more than I can stand. I take authority over temptation now! I command every tempting thought and suggestion made by the enemy to cease their maneuvers against me. I reject temptation and I know that God will show me a way to endure it. Lord, I thank You for I will never face any temptation that I cannot overcome.

Psalm 119:37 (NIV)

Turn my eyes away from worthless things; preserve my life according to your word.

Declaration 2: I Have Victory over Temptation

Holy Spirit, turn my eyes from worthless things and teach me how to preserve my life according to Your Word. Thank You, Father, that I do not face temptation alone. You are with me and You will not let my foot slip as I flee from temptation. Holy Spirit, I thank You for leading me out of temptation and into victory. You always cause me to triumph.

I COMMIT MY APPETITE TO GOD

Psalm 37:5 (NLT)

Commit everything you do to the LORD. Trust him, and he will help you.

Declaration 1: I Commit my Appetite to God

Holy Father, I commit my appetite to You today, and I make food choices that will bless my body and not curse it. I command my appetite to submit to God's dietary plan for my life. I place every unhealthy desire and craving under God's authority and the Weight of His Word. I trust God to help me control my appetite and He will help me. Lord, thank You for Your power.

Psalm 103:1-5 (NIV)

Praise the Lord, my soul; all my inmost being, praise his holy name. Praise the Lord, my soul, and forget not all his benefits, who forgives all your sins and heals all your diseases, who redeems your life from the pit and crowns you with love and compassion, who satisfies your desires with good things so that your youth is renewed like the eagle's.

Declaration 2: I Commit my Appetite to God

Father, I praise you and I do not forget Your benefits of health and healing. You have redeemed my life from the sins of idolatry and gluttony and shown me Your love and compassion. I Thank You, Lord, for satisfying my desires and hunger with good things so that my youth is renewed like the eagles. God, thank You for forgiving all my sins and healing any diseases that try to curse my body.

I DO NOT EAT TO LIVE

Matthew 4:4 (NLT)

But Jesus told him, "No! The Scriptures say, 'People do not live by bread alone, but by every word that comes from the mouth of God.'"

Declaration: I Do Not Eat to Live

I do not live by bread alone. I partake of the bread of life and every word that comes from the mouth of God. I do *not* live to eat; I eat to protect my health and to live a long, healthy and whole life. Father, I thank You, for Your Word has filled me up.

I AM CONTENT

Philippians 4:11 (NIV)

I am not saying this because I am in need, for I have learned to be content whatever the circumstances.

Declaration 1: I Am Content

Holy Spirit, teach me to be content regardless of my current weight and circumstances. I pray that I will not confuse contentment with passivity so that I may do my part to overcome weight. Lord Jesus, thank you for providing all that I need to be content.

> *Proverbs 18:20 (NASB)*
>
> *With the fruit of a man's mouth his stomach will be satisfied; He will be satisfied with the product of his lips.*

Declaration 2: I Am Content

Father, I thank you for satisfying my entire being with the fruit of Your Word. My stomach will be satisfied with the fruit of my lips, for Your Word produces life and healing in my body, heart, and mind. Thank You, Lord; You have provided the bread of life, and I am satisfied with the harvest produced by Your words coming from my mouth.

I COMMAND MY BODY

> *Job 22:28*
>
> *Thou shalt also decree a thing, and it shall be established unto thee: and the light shall shine upon thy ways.*

Declaration 1: I Command My Body

Body, I speak gently to you because I love you. You hear me, and you will walk in obedience to all I command you. You shall obey my voice so that all will go well with you. Appetite, you will come into alignment with God's plan for me to be whole and well. Thank You, God, for giving power to the words I speak.

Declaration 2: I Command My Body

I speak to my thoughts, my will, and my heart: I command you to be on one accord, working together with my hands, feet, and my senses of smell, taste, and sight. In times of temptation; you will be victorious. God, thank You, for not allowing the members of my body to betray me for food. All my members are working together for my good health.

Declaration 3: I Command My Body

I command every part of my body to be well now; every cell, organ, muscle, and bone is whole and well. I call for every mental and emotional issue to be still and rest in the peace of God, now! Jesus, I thank You for dealing with depression, anxiety and emotional trauma at the cross. They have no hold on me for I curse them at the root. in Jesus' Name.

Declaration 4: I Command My Body

I declare that sickness and disease have no place in my body. I speak to obesity, diabetes, hypertension, heart attack, stroke, cancer, multiple sclerosis, lupus, sickle cell anemia, asthma, fibromyalgia and any other sickness or disease. You are *not* allowed to dwell in my body, and if you are present, the Lord Jesus rebukes you and you must leave my body now! Thank You, Jesus, for carrying every sickness and disease. I cry out to you for healing and restoration and you heal me.

Declaration 5: I Command My Body

I command my body to be the perfect weight for my frame and body type. I bind anything that will prohibit me from losing weight and being whole. I receive the wisdom of God that gives me clear direction to meet my weight release goals. God, I thank You for giving me the power to command my body weight to respond to Your Word.

THE WEIGHT IS OVER

>*Psalm 118:23 (NIV)*
>
>*The LORD has done this, and it is marvelous in our eyes.*

Declaration 1: The Weight is Over

Thank You Lord; finally, the weight is over! You have amazed me. I give You all the glory for You have brought me through. This is Your doing and it is marvelous in my eyes. I shall ever praise You God for delivering me from the weight that once had me bound. I am free.

>*Mark 10:27 (NLT)*
>
>*Jesus looked at them intently and said, "Humanly speaking, it is impossible. But not with God. Everything is possible with God."*

Declaration 2: The Weight is Over

Humanly speaking, weight loss was impossible for me; however, the anointed Word of God destroys every yoke of bondage and weight. Father, I put *Your* Word on my weight, and I see that permanent weight loss is possible. Your Word strengthens me, Your grace empowers me, and Your Spirit gives me the wisdom to overcome. My struggle with weight is over forever! Jesus, I thank and praise You, for You reign over every weight.

Glory to God! It Is Finished! The Weight is Over. I have the Victory!

Let's make this final declaration of faith: Who the Son sets free is free indeed! I am free because I have Put God's Word on my Weight. To God be the glory for this wonderful freedom that He has given me!

Amen and Amen.

END NOTES

1. Andrew Murray. *Humility: The Journey Toward Holiness.* Bethany House Publishers, 2001.

2. Ibid.

Published by:
PublishAffordably.com | 773.783.2981